Related Books of Interest

Viral Data in SOA
An Enterprise Pandemic

by Neal Fishman

ISBN-13: 978-0-13-700180-4

Leading IBM information forensics expert Neal Fishman helps you identify the unique challenges of data quality in your SOA environment—and implement solutions that deliver the best results for the long term at the lowest cost. Writing for both business and technical professionals, Fishman shows how to think about data quality on a risk/reward basis…establishing an effective data governance initiative…how to evaluate data quality and overcome its inevitable decay…and, last but not least, how to actually derive a data quality initiative that works.

SOA Governance
Achieving and Sustaining Business and IT Agility

by William A. Brown, Robert G. Laird, Clive Gee, and Tilak Mitra

ISBN: 978-0-13-714746-5

In *SOA Governance*, a team of IBM's leading SOA governance experts share hard-won best practices for governing IT in any service-oriented environment.

The authors begin by introducing a comprehensive SOA governance model that has worked in the field. They define what must be governed, identify key stakeholders, and review the relationship of SOA governance to existing governance bodies as well as governance frameworks like COBIT. Next, they walk you through SOA governance assessment and planning, identifying and fixing gaps, setting goals and objectives, and establishing workable roadmaps and governance deliverables. Finally, the authors detail the build-out of the SOA governance model with a case study.

Related Books of Interest

The New Language of Business
SOA & Web 2.0

By Sandy Carter

ISBN-13: 978-0-13-195654-4

In *The New Language of Business*, senior IBM executive Sandy Carter demonstrates how to leverage SOA, Web 2.0, and related technologies to drive new levels of operational excellence and business innovation.

Writing for executives and business leaders inside and outside IT, Carter explains why flexibility and responsiveness are now even more crucial to success — and why services-based strategies offer the greatest promise for achieving them.

You'll learn how to organize your business into reusable process components — and support them with cost-effective IT services that adapt quickly and easily to change. Then, using extensive examples — including a detailed case study describing IBM's own experience — Carter identifies best practices, pitfalls, and practical starting points for success.

 Listen to the author's podcast at:
ibmpressbooks.com/podcasts

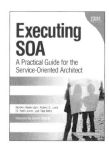

Executing SOA
A Practical Guide for the Service-Oriented Architect

by Norbert Bieberstein, Robert G. Laird, Dr. Keith Jones, and Tilak Mitra

ISBN-13: 978-0-13-235374-8

In Executing SOA, four experienced SOA implementers share realistic, proven, "from-the-trenches" guidance for successfully delivering the largest and most complex SOA initiative. This book follows up where the authors' best-selling *Service-Oriented Architecture Compass* left off, showing how to overcome key obstacles to successful SOA implementation and identifying best practices for all facets of execution—technical, organizational, and human. Among the issues it addresses include introducing a services discipline that supports collaboration and information process sharing; integrating services with preexisting technology assets and strategies; choosing the right roles for new tools; shifting culture, governance, and architecture; and bringing greater agility to the entire organizational lifecycle, not just isolated projects.

 Listen to the author's podcast at:
ibmpressbooks.com/podcasts

Related Books of Interest

Enterprise Master Data Management
An SOA Approach to Managing Core Information

Allen Dreibelbis, Eberhard Hechler, Ivan Milman, Martin Oberhofer, Paul van Run, and Dan Wolfson

ISBN-13: 978-0-13-236625-0

Enterprise Master Data Management provides an authoritative, vendor-independent MDM technical reference for practitioners: architects, technical analysts, consultants, solution designers, and senior IT decision makers. Written by the IBM® data management innovators who are pioneering MDM, this book systematically introduces MDM's key concepts and technical themes, explains its business case, and illuminates how it interrelates with and enables SOA.

Drawing on their experience with cutting-edge projects, the authors introduce MDM patterns, blueprints, solutions, and best practices published nowhere else—everything you need to establish a consistent, manageable set of master data, and use it for competitive advantage.

WebSphere Engineering
Ding
ISBN-13: 978-0-13-714225-5

IBM WebSphere System Administration
Williamson, Chan, Cundiff, Lauzon, Mitchell
ISBN-13: 978-0-13-144604-5

WebSphere Business Integration Primer
Iyengar, Jessani, Chilanti
ISBN-13: 978-0-13-224831-0

Rapid Portlet Development with WebSphere Portlet Factory
Bowley
ISBN-13: 978-0-13-713446-5

Enterprise Java Programming with IBM WebSphere, Second Edition
Brown, Craig, Hester, Pitt, Stinehour, Weitzel, Amsden, Jakab, Berg
ISBN-13: 978-0-321-18579-2

Service-Oriented Architecture (SOA) Compass
Bieberstein, Bose, Fiammante, Jones, Shah
ISBN-13: 978-0-13-187002-4

IBM WebSphere
Barcia, Hines, Alcott, Botzum
ISBN-13: 978-0-13-146862-7

Dynamic SOA and BPM

Dynamic SOA and BPM

Best Practices for Business Process Management and SOA Agility

Marc Fiammante

IBM Press
Pearson plc
Upper Saddle River, NJ • Boston • Indianapolis • San Francisco
New York • Toronto • Montreal • London • Munich • Paris • Madrid
Cape Town • Sydney • Tokyo • Singapore • Mexico City

ibmpressbooks.com

IBM Press Program Managers: Steven Stansel, Ellice Uffer
Cover design: IBM Corporation

Associate Publisher: Greg Wiegand
Marketing Manager: Kourtnaye Sturgeon
Acquisitions Editor: Katherine Bull
Publicist: Heather Fox
Development Editor: Kendell Lumsden
Managing Editor: Kristy Hart
Designer: Alan Clements
Project Editor: Anne Goebel
Copy Editor: Geneil Breeze
Indexer: Lisa Stumpf
Compositor: Jake McFarland
Proofreader: Sheri Cain
Manufacturing Buyer: Dan Uhrig

Published by Pearson plc
Publishing as IBM Press

IBM Press offers excellent discounts on this book when ordered in quantity for bulk purchases or special sales, which may include electronic versions and/or custom covers and content particular to your business, training goals, marketing focus, and branding interests. For more information, please contact:

> U. S. Corporate and Government Sales
> 1-800-382-3419
> corpsales@pearsontechgroup.com

For sales outside the U. S., please contact:

> International Sales
> international@pearsoned.com

Library of Congress Cataloging-in-Publication Data

Fiammante, Marc.

  Dynamic SOA and BPM : best practices for business process management and SOA agility/Marc Fiammante.

        p. cm.

  ISBN-13: 978-0-13-701891-8 (hardback : alk. paper)

  ISBN-10: 0-13-713084-8 (hardback : alk. paper) 1. Service oriented architecture (Computer science) 2. Business--Data processing. 3. Industrial management--Data processing. 4. Business logistics--Data processing. I. Title.

  TK5105.5828.F53 2009

  658.500285--dc22

                                                                                          2009020223

ISBN-13: 978-0-13-701891-8

ISBN-10: 0-13-701891-6

Text printed in the United States on recycled paper at R.R. Donnelley in Crawfordsville, Indiana.

First printing July 2009

This book was written in memory of Jason Weisser, a true friend, who used to affectionately call me "mon ami." Jason led the IBM SOA Advanced Technology team, where I first met him, and afforded me the opportunity to build the knowledge base and experience that I've shared in this book.

Deep love to my wife, Corine, and daughter, Florence, for the support they provided me during this long effort and for accepting the significant amount of time it required of our family life.

Contents

Foreword

Confronted by competitive pressures and the worst economic climate in decades, today's enterprises need to be increasingly focused on leveraging SOA and BPM to meet their business objectives and capitalize on market opportunities. With mashups and Web 2.0 capabilities becoming ever more prevalent, SOA has reached a level of pervasiveness that requires businesses to quickly adapt. Nowhere is the need more evident than with the millions of mobile workers who toil each day outside the bounds of the traditional enterprise. These workers depend on their devices to consume services and enable business processes cleanly and efficiently while being flexible enough to integrate behavior and business logic changes without requiring new deployments; they expect changes in backend enterprise systems to be totally opaque.

Approaches that increase flexibility help limit the impact on the consuming side when changes are made on the provider side, which leads to greater business value, better development practices, and faster time to market. Dexterra is leading enterprise mobility by example. At Dexterra, we embrace service-orientation in building composite mobile solutions that deliver SOA and BPM best practices to help demanding companies automate previously manual processes, empower employees with the information they need to improve job performance, and transform the enterprise with real-time visibility and control. Our Dexterra Concert mobile platform embodies this SOA approach to enable enterprises to drive dramatic improvements in productivity, performance, flexibility, and responsiveness.

Marc Fiammante is a proven authority on the topic of SOA, having spent years leading field projects and delivering SOA and BPM adaptability. The insights he has accumulated in this book make it an extremely useful asset and reference point for enterprises looking to implement or gain greater value from their SOA and BPM strategy and to extend the capability to workers of all types, mobile or not.

—**Michael S. Liebow**
  CEO, Dexterra

Acknowledgments

I thank the IBM® management team for allowing me the time necessary to write this book. All books written at IBM receive full support from management. I'd like to thank my executive sponsors at IBM Software Group, especially Doug Hunt, vice president, SOA Advanced Technologies; Ed Kahan, IBM fellow, SOA Advanced Technologies; and Hervé Rolland, vice president, IBM Software Group France. I am also grateful for access to the resources needed to complete this project.

I offer a big thank you to Kendell Lumsden, my development editor, for her excellent advice. To Katherine Bull and Pearson Education, I offer my thanks for the strong support they've provided me during this effort.

Also, many thanks to Anthony Carrato, Olivier Casile, Paul Ashley, and Robert G. Laird, my reviewers on this book and esteemed colleagues.

About the Author

Marc Fiammante is an IBM distinguished engineer and worldwide chief architect of the SOA engagements delivered by the SOA Advanced Technology team. Marc has been a member of the IBM Academy of Technology since 2003 and has a 25-year background in IT, with extensive experience in large project architecture and software development on multiple environments. He leads architecture teams in major industries projects, particularly in telco and banking. He has filed several software domain patents, is coauthor of *Service-Oriented Architecture Compass* and has published several articles related to IT.

Marc has architectural and technical expertise and experience with SOA, Web Services, Enterprise Application Integration, e-business, and object-oriented technologies, including a number of software middlewares, programming languages, and standards.

From Simplified Integration to Dynamic Processes

He that will not apply new remedies must expect new evils; for time is the greatest innovator.

Francis Bacon

Common Pitfalls Limiting the Value of SOA and BPM

When Services Oriented Architecture (SOA) was initiated, the simplified integration capabilities brought hopes of a simplified business and IT landscape with reusable business components enabled by open technologies. A few years later, the results are uneven; some have experienced substantial benefits from a move to SOA, while others experienced more average value, even though they've used the appropriate technologies.

There are multiple reasons for not realizing the full business value of this services approach. Let's look at three essential reasons:

- **Many projects simply use advanced technologies to implement a client/server approach on Web Services**—Even though the protocol and technical adaptation is no longer a problem, they faced the same issues as a decade ago: changes to the server interfaces leading to client changes. My team faced such a scenario when a large bank decided to expose all its mainframe transactions as Web Services, but the operation semantic remained the same as for mainframe transactions. This pure bottom-up approach did not bring much business value, and in some cases, it led to worse performance.

- **Business processes reintroduce the tight coupling of flexible business services**—In many cases, Business Process Management (BPM) has been established as a disconnect approach from the SOA approach in which business services were limited to the exposure of existing application functions. This model fails to address the modularization and variability of the business processes, and the processes act like glue rigidifying the services. For example, a large telecommunications operator implemented an end-to-end order management in a very large, single Business Process Execution Language (BPEL), including more than 300 activities, and ultimately faced a lack of reusability when some sequences could have been modularized and exposed as services.

• **Rigid information models are used to expose business services**—In many cases, services are only viewed as operations, forgetting that the business information structure they carry will vary as well with the evolution of the business. For example, another telecommunication operator was updating its product catalog weekly and generating a new schema at each change. This led to instability of the exposed services and integration processes, and delayed IT projects rather than enabling faster cycles.

Each of these experiences induced a deeper thinking process. What should be the essence of a business variable approach? How can we reach a true business/IT alignment with the expected shortened IT cycle enabling faster and cheaper business reactions?

How Other Industries Approach Varying Conditions

The IT industry is not the first industry to face varying conditions. Even though computing technology itself has had some approaches to variability in the past, such as overloading or rules engines, here we expose some solutions for which we can find an implementation analogy in the IT industry.

Whether it is in the automotive industry with shock absorbers and suspension, or the building industry with expansion joints, or the mechanical industry with washers, a mediation layer always absorbs the variations of one part without affecting the other part. In these industries, the integrated elements may not need to vary or move internally, but at the end, a dynamic assembly is realized with tightly coupled parts flexibly linked with other parts. Components can be subassemblies with their own internal variability using similar technologies, but the higher level assembler only cares about the external characteristics of the components. Similarly, in the IT approach, there must be a notion of the levels of assembly and the granularity of components.

In all industries, the final assembly is designed based on a global architecture that looks at requirements, operating conditions, and desired capabilities. Dynamicity is not a goal by itself; it has to respond to a specific context and desired states. Take for instance, buildings in Tokyo, which require more flexibility to withstand earthquakes than buildings in Paris. A 4x4 car has to absorb more landscape variations than a limo. Similarly, the enterprise and business architects must look at how the enterprise business model needs to evolve and what market conditions it will face to understand the variability necessary.

A bank we worked with had to implement higher controls on its loan origination processes because of the Sarbanes-Oxley requirements. However, this bank operates in four different countries with four different legislations and four different IT systems. In addition, this bank plans to expand to Eastern Europe in the future. This specific case led to a common process trunk with variable subprocesses handling specific legislative constraints and a common top-down but variable services definition for account, products, customer information, and so on.

A Streamlined Enterprise Architecture for BPM and SOA

Every industry creates plans to address new markets, customers, or products. Similarly, such a business plan is required for an IT-enabled industry to identify potential evolutions and targeted domain boundaries. Such planning is essential to define which of the components will be tightly coupled as well as where and to what extent flexibility is necessary.

Merging the business strategy, implementation, information, and infrastructure aspects in a single enterprise architecture map is a common pitfall. Good architecture involves separation of concerns. Wikipedia provides a good definition of enterprise architecture that clearly separates the concerns:

> The architecture process addresses documenting and understanding the discrete enterprise structural components, typically within the following four categories: Business, Applications, Information, and Technology.[1]

In a dynamic enterprise approach using BPM and SOA, each domain requires a specific mapping and domain decomposition leading to a four-layer view of the enterprise with a simple mean to remember them.

There are recognized enterprise architecture frameworks or metamodels in the industry, such as The Open Group Architecture Framework (TOGAF)[2] and the Zachman Framework.[3] TOGAF is a method that addresses reification of the enterprise architecture (A to H) and the "why" (requirements), but does not separate as clearly as the Zachman Framework the "what," "how," "where," "who," and "when." The business information domain is covered by the "what," the business logic and functions performed are described by the "how," the various locations and topologies where the enterprise performs business are analyzed in the "where," the enterprise organization and the various actors are formalized in the "who," the events and dynamics of the business flows are modeled in the "when," and finally, the enterprise goals and requirement are captured in the "why."

However, a fully fledged enterprise architecture with an exhaustive approach for each of the preceding layers is perceived as a costly and lengthy process that does not always provide quick wins and pragmatic results. Applying these methods and frameworks to their full extent for an enterprise can be important; however, in a dynamic BPM and SOA approach, we need to apply a streamlined approach that is affordable and still has the necessary architectural models and work products.

The four domains—Business, Applications, Information, and Technology—are particularly important to an SOA and BPM approach as business processes consume business services exposed from applications or other business process modules. These business services apply functions on core business entities and information that allow their flexible integration at the enterprise level. The applications also consume technical services from the infrastructure layer. *Technical services* refer to services that do not pertain to a particular business domain but are common technical functions made available by the IT to the application layer. Examples of these technical services are "send eMail," "audit interaction," and so on. Each of these four domains has policies that define the rules and regulations that apply to a particular domain.

Figure 1-1 shows these four domain layers creating a mnemonic structure (a capital "E"). The top layer addresses business, the middle layer the applications (including the service components that they package), the bottom layer the infrastructure, and all are connected vertically by information, or in other words, the business logic.

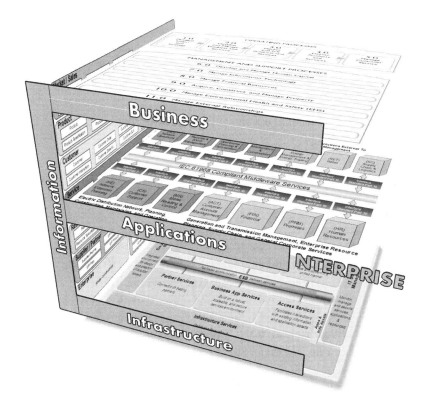

Figure 1-1   Mnemonic for the "E"nterprise architecture layers

In Chapter 2, "Streamlining the Enterprise Architecture for Dynamic BPM and SOA," we address techniques to achieve an efficient approach including horizon based enterprise architecture, enterprise architecture staged zooming, and accelerated implementations using template business and technical architectures.

But first, let's take a high-level view of the four enterprise architecture layers by looking at the business aspects.

Mapping the Enterprise Business

The use of an enterprise map in a dynamic BPM approach allows you to identify the boundaries of process modules that will have value for the enterprise. The detailed practice is discussed in subsequent chapters of this book. In this chapter, we look at bridging the enterprise architecture with this business modularization.

It is essential to identify the business components that deliver business capabilities and act as service centers in the enterprise that have the potential to operate independently. These components deliver value to the enterprise through their ability to deliver a unique set of business capabilities.

The need to operate independently necessitates that a business component be at the intersection of several axes, which could potentially include

- A business area or a decomposition of a business area
- An organizational structure operating within a business area
- An accountability level
- Business life cycle phases

Based on these different views, there are several approaches for defining a business map, the business components, and the business model. However, they all provide a decomposition of the business of an enterprise. A business process map is the static landscape on which business processes and business events provide dynamic behavior. A few standards are available, and in the next sections, we walk through some public examples of such enterprise maps and decompositions.

NGOSS Business Process Framework (eTOM)[4]

The enhanced Telecom Operations Map (eTOM) from the New Generation Operations Systems and Software (NGOSS) standard provides a business process functional decomposition framework for telecommunication service providers and serves as a neutral reference point and blueprint for decomposing processes to a level 3 of a functional decomposition tree. In Figure 1-2, you have a first level of decomposition with the verticals such as Fulfillment and an orthogonal first level of decomposition, Customer Relationship Management. At their intersection, there will be further decomposition in level 2 process catalogs such as Order Handling, which itself contains a further decomposition into a level 3 modularization.

This top-level map is complemented with a level 3 functional decomposition in the 300+ paged GB921D document, "The Business Process Framework (eTOM)."

Even though the standard says in business process decomposition no workflows are standardized, only a static functional decomposition of the business operations is provided. This is a good starting point, but the telecommunications business is highly dynamic, and static workflows are necessary for the modularization but insufficient for real business operations.

APQC Process Classification Framework[5]

The APQC (American Productivity and Quality Center, although now worldwide) is a standards body developed a classification of enterprise most common processes and captured that classification as a common language and open standard.

Particularly the classification looks at decomposition of the enterprise into finer grained elements and creating a tree of four levels, where each level addresses a particular semantic of the enterprise business (see Figure 1-3).

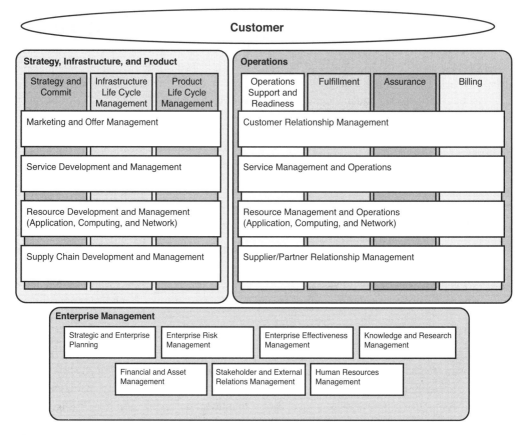

Figure 1-2   The Enhanced Telecom Operations Map (eTOM)

The Process Classification Framework (PCF) includes process groups and more than 1,500 processes and associated activities down to a level 4 of decomposition.

An essential aspect of the PCF is that it provides a standard for naming the different levels, which interestingly enough can be matched with the three eTOM levels. Similarly, even though the level 4 activities are usually sequential, there is no workflow standardization in the PCF.

These four levels are

1. **Categories**—Classifying business competency domains of the enterprise

2. **Process Group**—Grouping processes in business components that apply to similar business entities

3. **Process**—Formalized list of tasks and activities required to achieve a specific aspect of a business component

4. **Activity**—The granular business definition of an element that is chained by a higher level process.

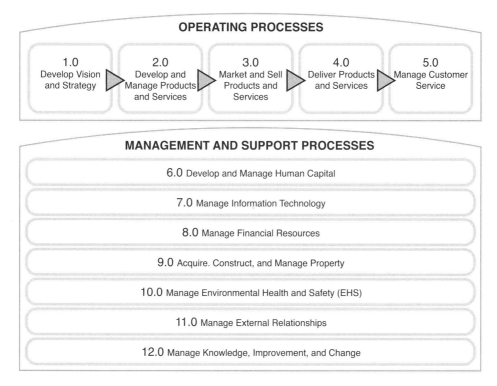

OPERATING PROCESSES

| 1.0 Develop Vision and Strategy | 2.0 Develop and Manage Products and Services | 3.0 Market and Sell Products and Services | 4.0 Deliver Products and Services | 5.0 Manage Customer Service |

MANAGEMENT AND SUPPORT PROCESSES

6.0 Develop and Manage Human Capital

7.0 Manage Information Technology

8.0 Manage Financial Resources

9.0 Acquire. Construct, and Manage Property

10.0 Manage Environmental Health and Safety (EHS)

11.0 Manage External Relationships

12.0 Manage Knowledge, Improvement, and Change

Figure 1-3   The PCF organizes processes into 12 enterprise-level categories.

This classification serves as the basis for further discussions in this book, particularly in the business service granularity discussion.

IBM®'s Component Business Modeling[6]

This approach from IBM is a new way of looking at an enterprise business. The Component Business Modeling (CBM) methodology identifies the basic building blocks of an enterprise business, as shown in Figure 1-4, to help address the future challenges of the enterprise.

This map is a mean to identify business components and create a business strategy for the enterprise. These business components have functionality that occurs once within the enterprise, and they act as business service centers that have the potential to operate independently. This enables the replacement of one business component by another implementation. For example, the product fulfillment can be delivered by many factories around the world, but the enterprise expects the same services from all product fulfillment instantiations around the globe. In one country or for one given product, the enterprise can own the factory while in another country, it can be a contractor. However, each business component delivers value to the enterprise through its ability to deliver a unique set of common services per business component function.

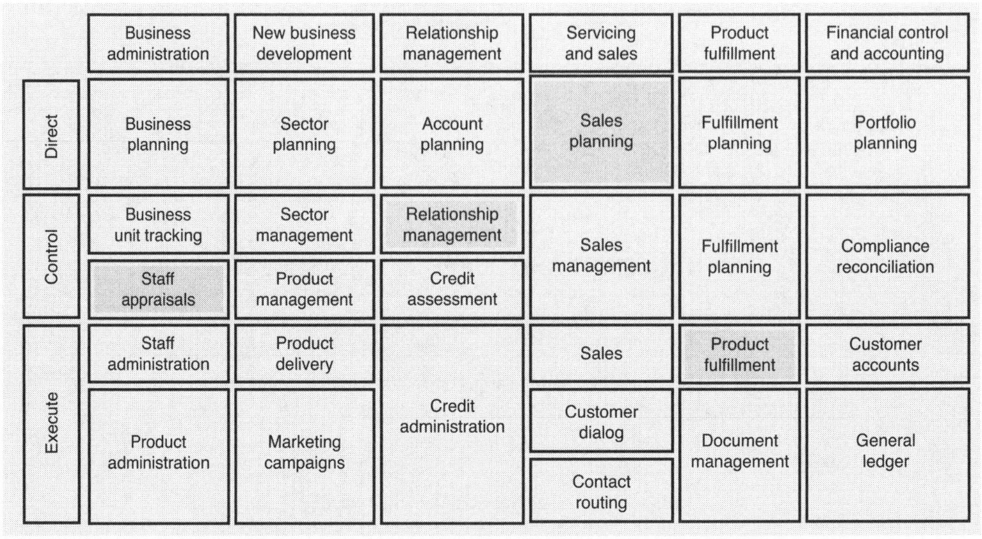

Business administration	New business development	Relationship management	Servicing and sales	Product fulfillment	Financial control and accounting
Direct Business planning	Sector planning	Account planning	Sales planning	Fulfillment planning	Portfolio planning
Control Business unit tracking / Staff appraisals	Sector management / Product management	Relationship management / Credit assessment	Sales management	Fulfillment planning	Compliance reconciliation
Execute Staff administration / Product administration	Product delivery / Marketing campaigns	Credit administration	Sales / Customer dialog / Contact routing	Product fulfillment / Document management	Customer accounts / General ledger

Figure 1-4   CBM map showing basic business building blocks

The implication is that explicit processes operate within the boundaries of a business component and use other business components' services to chain into the realization of processes that span the enterprise.

The granularity of business components is, however, often too high. In a dynamic process approach, these maps serve as the basis for further functional decomposition, and they can be considered as level 1 and level 2 of the APQC Process Classification Framework.

SCOR—The Supply-Chain Council

The Supply-Chain Council is a nonprofit global independent organization, composed of many companies around the world, which has produced the Supply-Chain Operations Reference (SCOR) model. This model is a process reference model that integrates the best practices for supply-chain operations business process reengineering.

SCOR addresses five distinct business domains called **management processes**, which are plan, source, make, deliver, and return.

In addition, the Council defines four levels of decomposition but only addresses the first three levels in the standard. The fourth level is the business differentiator of each company.

These four levels are

1. **Process Type**—This level 1 or top level provides a balanced cross business domains and cross process categorization. It defines the scope and content of the previously mentioned management processes.

2. **Process Category**—This level 2 or configuration level provides a reconfigurable level that companies will adjust to their own business plans.

3. **Process Element**—This level 3 or process element level contains the process modules that operate within a business component and can be reconfigured to achieve the higher level processes.

4. **Activities**—This level 4 or implementation level contains the necessary tasks and granular business services. SCOR standard considers this level to be specific to each and every enterprise and does not standardize this level.

Process model decomposition appears as a common practice among the publicly available models and standards. They do not all use the exact same terminology, but they all tend to modularize the representation of the business as a hierarchy and sequences of lower sets of business tasks.

As a confirmation that tree decompositions can be applied to process decomposition let me quote "A Coordination-Theoretic Approach to Understanding Process Differences" from MIT Sloan School of Management to show that derivation trees are common ways of designing processes for modularity and reusability:

> By applying top-down coordination-theoretic modeling, supported by a handbook of generic coordination mechanisms and exceptions handlers, we were able to create derivation trees for all three processes that made the source of their similarities and differences much easier to identify.[7]

Usually significant variations appear below the third level of decomposition in being consistent with APQC at the task level defined by its categorization.

Defining Service Granularity from Business Maps

My customers frequently ask, "What is a good service granularity?" Business maps and decompositions are a particularly powerful tool to identify a service granularity and, thus, answer this question. I regularly use them in customer meetings and receive excellent feedback.

However, to answer this question, first we need to precisely define a service. In the following discussion and throughout this book, we use these definitions:

- **Business service**—The grouping of repeatable business tasks that address the same functional domain, for example, Process Customer Order. Business policies are defined at this business service level, such as policies to handle various business services for corporate customers or individuals. The term we use is specifically looking at software components that deliver business logic and not business activities at the level of "sell cars" or "provide mobile telephone services."

- **Web Service**—A technical representation of the elements of a business service, grouping discrete business tasks together for technical management such as versioning in a technical descriptor using either Web Services Description Language (WSDL) or in a more abstract fashion Service Component Architecture (SCA) as technical standards. Looking at the Process Customer Order business service, the included Web Services might be Customer Order Life Cycle Management and Customer Order Information Management. There can be one or more Web Services per business service, but in many cases there will be only one.

- **Service operation**—A repeatable business task. In the previous case, a service operation might be Perform Order Feasibility Check, Submit Customer Order, or Receive Order Status Update. These are usually qualified as operations in the WSDLs or SCA descriptors. The number of operations range from one to ten or more. Given these definitions, let's do a simple computation. At a level 2, an enterprise usually has between 50 to 100 business components or process groups. Down one level, there are between 300 and 1,000 processes in the enterprise. For example, the eTOM telecommunication business process decomposition gives around 400 processes at level 3.

  At level 4, the number of tasks will be between 1,000 and 10,000. APQC has 1,500 activities defined at level 4, and if we pushed eTOM to a further decomposition, at a level 4 we have around five to seven times 400, or 2,500 tasks.

  We see that this is already a very large number of tasks, and a large portion of these tasks can potentially become business services. If we compute the number of operations, this gives us a potential of 5,000 to 20,000 service operations for the enterprise, a huge effort to manage. However, only a fraction of the enterprise has value to be exposed as business services and processes, and from our experience between 1% and 5% of the potential services operation has reusability value at the enterprise line of business levels.

The conclusions on granularity are

1. A good business service granularity, to maintain value and manageability, is between level 3 and level 4 of the enterprise functional decomposition. This usually corresponds to the APQC level 4, Activities.

2. Without a functional decomposition, there is no way to know the granularity level of a given service.

3. Processes should be modularized using a functional decomposition to make the modules reusable as business services at level 3. At level 4 or under, the business services are exposed from applications as detailed in the section, "Mapping the Enterprise Applications," later in the chapter.

4. Any too fine-grained Application Programming Interface (API) at level 5 or below should be aggregated into a coarser grained service by applying variability on the interfaces and resolving the variability between the façade and the API.

Mapping the Enterprise Applications

There is a difference between the business components and the implementation of the services that they require. Let' look at a concrete example.

At level 3 eTOM defines a Track and Manage Order Handling process, part of the Order Handling group. However this process requires accessing services from a Customer Information Management, a Product Catalog Management, a Billing Management, and a Customer Order Life Cycle Management application, which is implementing the services.

If the intention is to look at a future state architecture, the **ideal application map** must be defined. This is the map that an enterprise would create if there were no financial, time, or technology restrictions. These maps are often delivered by IT consulting companies and often referred to as "city planning." This application map is the superstructure of interfaces that will be exposed as the reusable business services layer.

Defining these maps in a top-down approach is essential to isolate the business processes that consume services from the real implementations in the existing applications. This top-down approach needs to be complemented by a bottom-up approach that defines how existing or new applications and packages will be adapted to expose these interfaces in a flexible and consistent manner. The best practices for delivering such adaptations are discussed in later chapters of this book.

One standards body standardizes this application map, and it's no surprise the TeleManagement Forum (TmForum) is the most advanced in that space, as telecommunication operators are faced with exponential growth and dynamic market evolutions, requiring higher levels of standardization for lowering costs.

TmForum Telecom Applications Map[8]

The Telecom Applications Map provides the bridge between the NGOSS standardized business process and information framework building blocks (eTOM and the SID, Shared Information and Data model) and real, deployable, potentially procurable applications by grouping together process functions and information data into recognized operation support and business support applications or services.

Even though no standard can ever represent a perfect systems infrastructure for an operator, the map provided in Figure 1-5 presents a functional and information guideline for implementing a layer of reusable business services exposed by application.

Mapping the Enterprise IT Infrastructure

The business processes and applications require an IT and middleware infrastructure to operate. It is important that this infrastructure also provides support for variability and flexibility at a core technical level. Even though some standards like the Open Grid Services Infrastructure (OGSI)[9] are looking at standardizing services exposed from infrastructure components, there are no commonly accepted standards for middleware and operating systems services.

One approach to a product-agnostic map is the SOA Reference Model that IBM provides. This model, shown in Figure 1-6, serves as a reference point to position both middleware and functionality within a service-oriented architecture. For further details, see "IBM SOA Foundation: An Architectural Introduction and Overview."[10]

Mapping the Enterprise Information

Information is the essential "logical" asset that links together all layers of the enterprise. As processes do not run in vacuum but carry, transform, and refer to information, the structure of that information reflects the way the enterprise wants to operate. Figure 1-7 shows how telecommunication operators relate business domains to core entity domains.

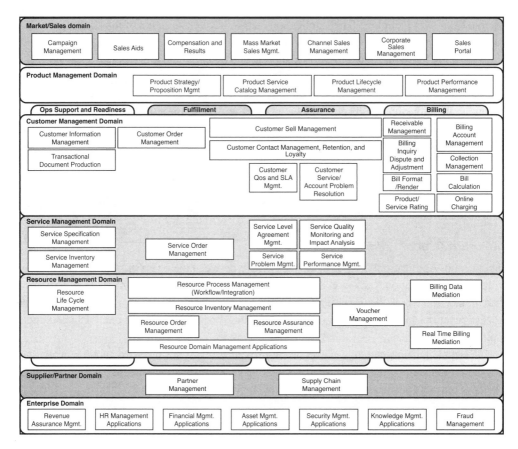

Figure 1-5   The TmForum Telecommunication Application Map GB929 R2.1

The business information model, domain maps, and core entities represent the business view of the information as opposed to data models, which address the technical implementation of managed objects data (see IETF RFC 3444[11]).

As an example of the influence of business on the information model, let's look at a retailer that used to sell single products and now wants to sell bundles. Should the bundle business object be considered a product with its own pricing superseding included products, or should it be another type of business entity with a global pricing deduced by applying discounts to the products included in the bundle? This is typically a business question that relies on the business model and needs to be reflected in the information model.

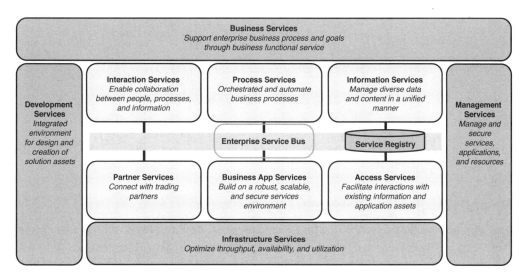

Figure 1-6 The IBM SOA Foundation Reference Model

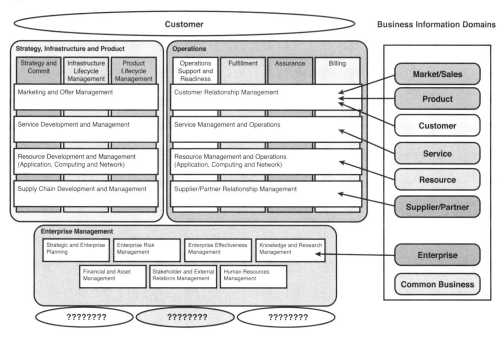

Figure 1-7 TeleManagement Forum eTOM and SID relationships

The Unified Modeling Language (UML) diagram in Figure 1-8 shows inheritance on the left or none on the right, a consequence of the way the enterprise intends to address markets.

A question arises: Can we make the model flexible enough to address both cases and allow variations of the business model in the future? We address approaches to a realization of this variability in Chapter 3, "Implementing Dynamic Enterprise Information."

Figure 1-8   Business model affecting the information model

Basic Principles for Enterprise Dynamicity

Now that we have set the static scene for the enterprise architecture, how do we use all these elements in a way that allows a dynamic business and IT approach? Dynamicity implies flows and movements, with events and messages propagating through the enterprise and variations between and within the business components. Flows, such as the Order to Bill, flow across enterprise components and are often referred to as **end-to-end processes**. However, it is essential to differentiate the apparent effect of an event's chain reaction from an explicit choreography of business services owned by a specific organization within the enterprise. Both are called business processes but are different in nature and implementation.

To differentiate these business processes, we use business decompositions and map to a common terminology with a precise definition of the different types of processes at each level. For this purpose, we use the categorization of basic types of processes derived from the Business Process Modeling Notation (BPMN) standard.

Categorizing the Processes

The BPMN standard introduces three basic types of submodels within an end-to-end BPMN model:[12]

1. **Collaboration (global) processes**—Business to business between enterprises or organizations

2. **Abstract (public) processes**—Inside an enterprise across business components or internal organizations

3. **Private (internal) business processes**—Within business components

In addition, BPMN introduces the notions of **pools** and **lanes**, which are also helpful in decomposing processes in modules and grains, allowing them to then be articulated in a flexible and dynamic fashion.

Collaboration (Global) Processes

A collaboration process is the description of the interactions between two completely independent business entities. Cross-industry standards, such as ebXML BPSS, RosettaNet, or to some extent, industry-specific standards, such as ACORD, describe such interactions sequences. The example collaboration process in Figure 1-9 shows a sequence of purchase order processing between two companies.

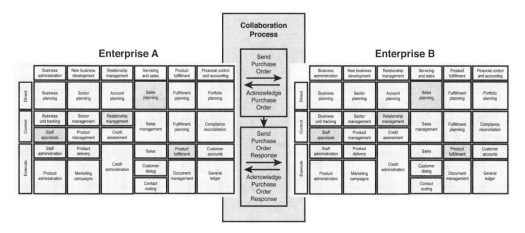

Figure 1-9 Example collaboration process

Even though there is a formal sequence, there is not an engine between the enterprises orchestrating that sequence. Each company/enterprise is responsible for sequencing its own part within its boundaries. EDI VANs are an early form of these collaboration processes, which are progressively disappearing because they inhibited flexibility.

Abstract (Public) Processes

These processes represent the overall interactions between different internal organizations in the enterprise owning their internal business rules or sequences. Consequently, abstract processes do not have a single business owner and would not be easily manageable if implemented as a single IT construct.

A first, obvious level of abstract processes is between business components as defined previously, but looking at the APQC decomposition, these abstract processes also occur between the processes at level 3 of the Process Classification Framework. Just as for the collaboration processes, there cannot be an engine controlling the interactions between the business components or level 3 processes because there would not be an owner of the logic in that engine. The overall sequence is the result of services calls and events occurring between each of the level 3 processes or business components. Understanding this difference between an explicit control and an implicit realization of the business process is essential to understanding the approach for implementing dynamic business processes.

In Figure 1-10, the "sales to bill" abstract process is represented by the interactions between the business components.

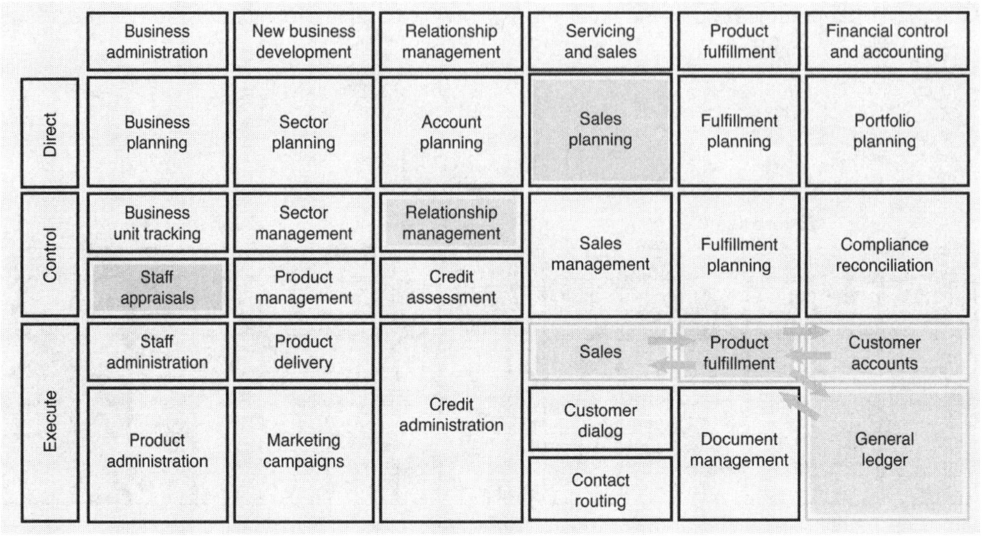

	Business administration	New business development	Relationship management	Servicing and sales	Product fulfillment	Financial control and accounting
Direct	Business planning	Sector planning	Account planning	Sales planning	Fulfillment planning	Portfolio planning
Control	Business unit tracking	Sector management	Relationship management	Sales management	Fulfillment planning	Compliance reconciliation
	Staff appraisals	Product management	Credit assessment			
Execute	Staff administration	Product delivery		Sales	Product fulfillment	Customer accounts
	Product administration	Marketing campaigns	Credit administration	Customer dialog	Document management	General ledger
				Contact routing		

Figure 1-10   Abstract sales to bill process

Private (Internal) Business Processes

Within a single organization with a single identified business owner, the owner can manage the rules and sequences of tasks, which are then private to that "owner" or his delegates.

As a result, private processes are preferable for explicit flow control and automation because they are manageable assets of the enterprise, for which stake holders and life cycle can define.

They can be either explicit, if expressed in a workflow language or service choreography/orchestration language such as XML Process Definition Language (XPDL) or Web Services Business Process Execution Language (BPEL), or implicit, if resulting from the code running inside a particular application or package such as the ones provided by companies like SAP, Oracle, Amdocs, and so on. These processes chain to other private processes either by the means, events, or services calls. If they are exposed as services and consume services, they then can become components in an assembly model, such as standardized by the Service Component Architecture standard from the Open SOA organization.[13] These private processes match the APQC processes that are at decomposition level 3. They operate within the boundaries of a business component, and there can be several private processes in a given business component or within a finer grained decomposition. Figure 1-11 shows an SCA assembly diagram where the customer order process (ProcessCustomerOrder) is exposed as a service and consumes other services, one of which is another process validating the customer order.

This private process is exposed from within the eTOM level 3 as shown in Figure 1-12.

As you can see the service component in Figure 1-11 has more interfaces than the level 3 of the process decomposition in Figure 1-12, highlighting the difference between a component providing an implementation in the application map and a private process identified from the process decomposition.

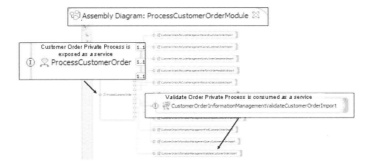

Figure 1-11   Private process exposed as a component and consuming other processes

Figure 1-12   Private process in eTOM level 3

Pools/Lanes

Within a private process, a **lane** represents a sequence of tasks or activities driven by a specific participant. A participant can be any specific party role such as a buyer, seller, or call center operator, but also it can be a technical participation such a bus mediation or a program routine. The identification of a lane's nature has an impact on the selection of the appropriate technologies for implementing particular portions, services, or a private process. **Pools** are group of lanes and seem to imply multiple actors. However, this is not explicitly stated in the BPMN standard.

Applying Decomposition to End-to-End Process

As a consequence of decomposing processes in categories, an end-to-end process is the abstract or collaboration process resulting from the assembly of private processes that group the lanes that interact within their boundaries.

Here is an example or "order to cash" end-to-end abstract process for telecommunication operators, composed of a chain of private processes contained within the boundaries of a business component.

In Figure 1-13, we identify variations of private processes, such as the various service configurations and resource provisioning. This example also looks at private processes that are common successors in an abstract flow, such as the Set Top Box configuration required by the three services of a triple play—that is, Internet, television, and voice-over-IP calling services.

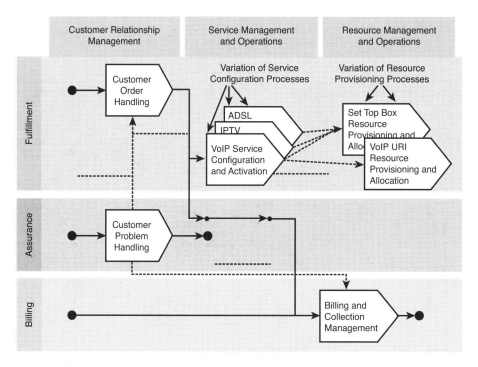

Figure 1-13   Abstract process of chaining private processes on a business map

In this specific case, the services can be submitServiceOrder with three implementations: submitServiceOrderForVoIP, submitServiceOrderForIPTV, and submitServiceOrderForADSL.

In a dynamic process approach, we must be able to add a quadruple play service such as gaming, with its specific service configuration and resources, without having to regenerate and test the "end to end" abstract process. This can only be achieved by means of dynamic binding and coordination between the various private processes.

Impact of Business Information Changes to Processes

The less you carry, the more agile you are. Similarly, the less information processes carry, the more they are able to handle variations of the enterprise information. But that information still needs to be accessible from the various business organizations of the enterprise, and the appropriate information must be available to the business components that require it for valid business needs.

To reach process agility, we have to move from a processes that carries explicitly all the information to processes that refer to information preserved elsewhere. Then, we only pass the core of the decisional information through processes, and preserve the bulk of the information using a master data management approach and information services to access that data as required by the business components and processes.

This still does not solve the variation of the interface to that information if attributes are added. An enterprise information variability approach is the necessary complement to ensure that within acceptable limits, the information model characteristics can change without affecting the interfaces.

The Enterprise Expansion Joint

This process and information dynamicity requires flexibility, and a mediation layer between components is one of the elements that provides such flexibility. The initial solution to the mediation layer in IT and a services-oriented architecture has been the Enterprise Services Bus. However, these buses often address the technical variability, looking at protocols and messaging, leaving the content interpretation to the integrated consumers or providers.

There is a need to push the mediation layer capabilities to content and business semantic adaptation, thus removing the interface's tight coupling of consumers and providers. As a simple example, the IT solution should enable the evolution of the versions of provided business services without requiring an immediate regeneration of business service consumers.

All the additional capabilities lead to what I call the **enterprise expansion joint**, the capacity for the business to expand using existing IT capabilities, without having to enter a long delivery process. The business variations of this expansion joint have to be bound to precisely identified limits that should be identified during the enterprise architecture phase. The enterprise architecture modeling method must then address the sizing of the business variability that this expansion layer can absorb, looking at foreseeable future business evolutions.

I had a concrete case where an enterprise wanted to deliver a new customer application and process while planning to change billing systems in a later phase. The target was to allow this change of billing systems for another packaged application without affecting any of the elements of the new customer care environment. So, the approach was to define what business services a billing system should expose to customer care in a top-down fashion and then use the mediation layer to perform the adaptation between exposed APIs and desired granularity and variability. In this specific case, the existing billing system was Tuxedo-based and required to use units of work in C for consistency, which led us to create a specific adapter, delivered in less than one month using the available adapter frameworks.

In addition to the granularity adaptation, the mediation layer may also have to address state as the reusable business services are designed to be independent of any implementation. Thus it may not expose specific data that is necessary for a specific application or package realizing the service.

In Chapter 6, "Implementing the Enterprise Expansion Joint," we discuss a set of techniques for realizing such a layer.

Summary

In this chapter, we saw multiple aspects for an enterprise to address to realize the value of a truly dynamic BPM and SOA approach. This realization requires structuring the business, defining the business goals to identify foreseeable business variation, mapping organizational ownership to process architecture, as well as structuring the business information. There is no "one size fits all" solution; however, a set of modeling steps and implementation techniques are part of an enterprise architecture approach and are discussed in Chapter 2.

CHAPTER 2

Streamlining the Enterprise Architecture for Dynamic BPM and SOA

Have a bias toward action—let's see something happen now. You can break that big plan into small steps and take the first step right away.

Indira Gandhi

Focusing the Enterprise Architecture on Variability

Enterprise architecture is often viewed as too conceptual and having too large a scope to be pragmatic and show rapid results. However, a controlled SOA and Business Process Management (BPM) approach, with the appropriate focus management, can enable a faster path to the alignment of business and IT. However, faster does not mean omitting essential elements. The approach can be exhaustive, performing modularizing processes with a controlled granularity, variability, and analysis at each step of the "why," "what," "how," "where," "who," and "when."

The enterprise capability strategy is an important step in enterprise architecture, but it is not the purpose of this book to address an enterprise strategy approach. For the purposes of this book, the strategy is considered to be preexisting. Still, among the strategic capabilities, it is important to identify the ones that require dynamicity.

From field experience, my team (hereafter referred to as "we") constructed a way to obtain quick value and implementation with a focused and progressive approach, using some rather simple principles to address the business, application, information, and infrastructure layers described in Chapter 1, "From Simplified Integration to Dynamic Processes."

To use an analogy, in the building industry expansion joints are only needed in the specific locations where variations are expected. Similarly for an enterprise, one must plan for expansion in specific areas. Some basic strategy and business requirement questions must be answered as the first step:

- Where should my enterprise be flexible? Which of the enterprise objectives requires accrued variability?

- What is the business priority of the enterprise that drives change? In what sequence can I expect changes? What conditions will evolve first?

- What is the benefit/risk ratio of implementing that variability? Is there an internal sponsor?

These questions are often answered in the enterprise architecture or business strategy function of the organization. If not, usually some high value focus capabilities and areas are easily identifiable. Once these focus areas are identified, the streamlined process can happen using simple techniques and principles. In the next section, we look at some of the enterprise capabilities that drive dynamicity within the architecture of services and business processes.

Enterprise Capabilities Driving Dynamic BPM and SOA

In this chapter, we limit our discussion to capabilities and requirements. We address implementing dynamic business processes and flexible services in later chapters. First, let's look at the two major categories of capabilities leading to dynamic BPM and SOA: the technical agility of the enterprise and the business agility of the enterprise.

Enterprise Technical Agility

Enterprise technical agility addresses the speed and the effectiveness of the IT organization to deliver new IT services at minimum cost. At this step of the discussion, it is essential to differentiate between an IT service and a software service (SOA).

- **Software service (SOA)**—A well-defined, self-contained software component that delivers or fulfills a specific business or IT function but does not depend on the context or state of other services, for example, Create Customer Order or Validate User Identity.

- **IT service**—An end user application or a feature delivered by an IT organization or IT service provider to its clients (within or outside the enterprise). For example, this could include mail services, directories, a portal, applications, or document shared space for specific teams.

An IT service may or may not use software services in the SOA sense. The use of software services stems from requirements such as the speed of integration and interchangeability of software component implementation for components that expose and consume software services.

From IT Agility Requirements to a Simplified Integration

Historically, integrating systems silos implemented with different technologies has been the first category of requirements, looking at system access and protocols matchmaking. This integration introduces requirements for security and manageability simplification that ease the control of the overall enterprise IT, including IT services and software services. The "why" must still be driven by business requirements, and we examine two examples of such requirements now.

The first example is one of the largest European providers of IT solutions to savings banks. They needed to simplify the way their client savings banks accessed the core banking systems. Each savings bank defines its client banking applications and technology, with different operating systems and technical requirements. The software services layer exposed the core banking applications running on a mainframe Customer Information Control System (CICS®)[1] transactional system with Web Services using variable interfaces, allowing different types of clients to integrate without requiring a specific interface and technology for each of the clients. The requirements were not simply protocol and technology isolation, but also core system life cycle isolation from client applications, to keep their clients from having to regenerate their applications each time the core banking systems functions evolved.

The second example, in which I was personally involved, involves a large telecommunication enterprise in an emerging country, created from the merger of a wire line and mobile operator. In the end, all the systems were doubled, including maintaining two different billing systems. The first business requirement was to create a new customer care portal that allowed customers to interact with their bills. The IT requirements were to integrate the two existing billing technologies in a unified way, allowing the phasing out of one billing system in the future without affecting the client applications. A top-down approach was used to define what SOA services a billing system should expose and then connect these interfaces to the existing systems so that the new client process and application would be independent of the implementation technology.

Even though IT may anticipate a technology blueprint for simplified integration and define some IT driven requirements, the specific use of these technical capabilities should always come from a business requirement, such as being able to access all the billing information from a single portal in the latter example.

IT Agility Requirements Leading to Software Components

IT organizations have long wanted to have palettes of software components just as electronic components do. These components both expose and consume services defined in a logical way, which enables the IT to drag and drop these components in development environments to build business logic, applications, and processes. Thus, the development tool is left to resolve the logical interface to physical implementation adaptation and matchmaking.

This category of IT requirements looks at creating business functions from an assembly line of existing software components, using common integration mechanisms and standardized component description mechanisms, allowing automation of matchmaking code generation, and speeding the implementation.

Even though the standards are available today from the Open SOA organization[2] and commonly available development environments support the component model, few enterprises formalize this type of requirement for their IT development strategy, nor does this requirement materialize in the RFPs that I see.

Enterprise Business Agility

This category of requirements is where the need for the real value of SOA and BPM is expressed. SOA and BPM target aligning business and IT to make the enterprise agile and responsive to market and operating environment changes.

Business Agility Requirements Leading to Business Services

The term **business service** can be defined in many ways. Let me clarify how business service is used in this book. In this SOA and BPM context, a business service is a coarse granularity task that can be automated, corresponding to what APQC process classification framework defines as activities (level 4) or SCOR defines as process elements.

The same business service behavior varies based on the context, contract, or content as follows:

- **Context**—Contains the conditions of access to the business service such as channel, role of the client of the service, time of the day, and so on

- **Contract**—Contains specific business or operating constraints, such as performance, security, traceability, or manageability

- **Content**—Defines the business content elements of the interaction, such as identification of a product, resource, or attribute that may require different processing of the task

APQC Cross Industry "5.2.3.1 Receive Customer Complaints" and SCOR "SR1.4: Schedule Defective Product Shipment" are examples of business services. Using this definition, it becomes obvious that these requirements are directly derived from a UML use case analysis. However, further analysis is required to identify the need for agility.

First, we need to determine the use case granularity and then position the use case in a materialized classification or decomposition. If you are using UML modeling, this materialization takes the form of a package structure that can be derived from an industry standard, such as APQC, SCOR, or eTOM,[3] as shown in Figure 2-1.

Figure 2-1   Positioning use cases in a classification or decomposition

Figure 2-1 shows that the nature of products a telecommunication operator will have to support in the future is highly variable because the market is also evolving quickly. There will be specific derived use cases for whatever product category the operator is selling or will sell, but there is a need for a higher level variable "performProductOrderFeasibility" use case, positioned at a level 4 of decomposition in the eTOM, which will be the use case with which other use cases interact to create a model that can absorb variations.

For each use case, the analysis process is to first look at context, contract, and content; then look at the business strategy; and finally, if the implied variations of any of these three elements cannot be bounded at enterprise architecture time, these use cases represent a business requirement for agile business services.

Agility Requirements Leading to Dynamic Business Process Management

The benefit of BPM is to formalize the sequence of business tasks to provide a consistent approach to business operations so that it supports predictability and manageability of the enterprise. There also are direct benefits of consistency in terms of staff education. But enterprise market and operating conditions always evolve, whether an intentional evolution such as international expansion to emerging countries, or unintentional such as some regulation changes. So there is a need to identify requirements for a level of consistency of sets of operations, and among these are subsets that are subject to variations.

Here's a concrete example: A European bank operating in four countries wanted a consistent loan origination process for all of the four countries. Even though there was a consistent end-to-end abstract process, as defined by BPMN,[4] the various private processes were subject to variations due to different local country legislations—for example, France requires a notary public to interact with the bank for real estate loans.

As this bank's strategy is to expand to other countries, there is an obvious agility requirement for dynamic processes that enable faster expansion. These business processes will also be materialized as use cases but at a higher level of an enterprise decomposition or classification, which is level 3 or higher of APQC, eTOM, or SCOR. Figure 2-2 shows the use case at the correct decomposition level.

Figure 2-2 Business process in a decomposition

Horizon Approach to Enterprise Architecture

Now that we have looked at identifying the specific requirements for agility, let's approach the enterprise architecture or modeling the business of the enterprise. Even though this chapter occurs after the discussion of requirements analysis, the business requirements analysis obviously needs elements of a business map and decomposition.

Is a complete business map required to address enterprise capability focus areas and requirements? No. However, all the other enterprise business areas and components that the focus areas interact with or affect must be identified. They aren't all affected with the same importance but still need to be clearly scoped.

This variation of the "point of view" approach, which includes distance notions, is what I call the **horizon approach**; what do I see from where I am standing, and how far from my concerns will I be if I move to a better position?

The Business Horizon

Let's take a concrete example in the airline industry. This airline company has several enterprise goals:

- Increase plane utilization
- Increase customer satisfaction
- Reduce airport operation and reduce staff education costs
- Reduce financial exposure

These objectives lead to a focus for a faster plane rotation around the world, and the focus area is what airlines call Ramp Control. Figure 2-3 shows the business horizon of Ramp Control.

Ramp Control is a business component that interacts closely with Spot Assignment, Check-in, Departure/Arrival Control, and Catering but needs fewer details from components that are farther away, such as Treasury & Risk Management or Crew Administration (the farther away the component, the fewer details are needed). In addition, in the different airports in which this airline operates, any of the business components, such as Catering, Baggage Handling, or Spot Assignment, with which the Ramp Control operates may be delivered by different enterprises.

Thus, instead of having to model up to 100 business components for a level 2 business map, the enterprise architect can concentrate on the focus Ramp Control component, with more detailed interactions with the six components in the close horizon and higher level interactions with more aggregated interaction information with the five components farther away.

We only need to work on the business capabilities and the information that these components expose externally. However, the distance factor leads to services that have variable information granularity for the same logical capability.

Ideally, a second focus component or a variation of the focus component helps in defining the right capability flexibility for reuse. Remember that when we look at the surface of the integrated business components, we see from the focus component to achieve the flexible coupling: We want to avoid "deeper thus tighter" integration in a dynamic enterprise.

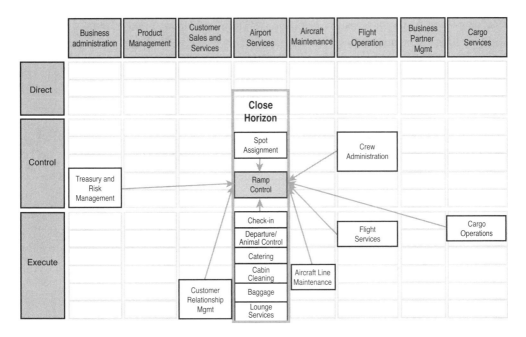

Figure 2-3   Ramp Control business map horizon

Information Horizon

Business components exchange information in their interactions. As we look at a horizon in the business mapping approach, we also need to look at the information from a horizon distance and integration perspective.

There is no one information model for the full enterprise. In the past years, there has been some focus on creating a canonical model as the pivot that would help integrate the enterprise. The reality is that there can be fewer (usually less than half a dozen). It is like a 3D view, with parallel and connected planes of information.

Here is an example in the telecommunication industry. Operators have prospects, which can turn into customers who buy products that contain telecommunication services using logical and physical resources. Product characteristics (for example, triple play with broadband Internet service, unlimited phone with Voice over IP [VoIP], and Television on IP [IPTV]) are transformed into service characteristics (bandwidth, mail box size) and resource characteristics (set top box, e-mail ID, VoIP URI). Figure 2-4 shows the relationship between the process managing the telco services problems and the telco service characteristic information.

The required level of detail on particular customers, products, services, or resources depends on our focus. Are we focusing on customer relationship management, telecommunication services management, or resources management?

The intersections between the information domain map and the business component map help in finding possible further information domain decompositions, starting from core entity domain at the enterprise level. Technically, this horizon approach ends up in a kind of relational denormalization of the information model, by splitting information and attributes by domain focus, creating secondary entities that are managed only by a given business component.

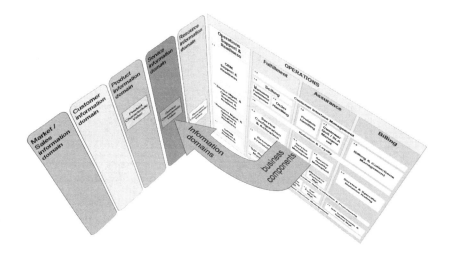

Figure 2-4   Intersecting telecommunication SID information and eTOM processes model

This information entity decomposition model is pursued until a single business owner is responsible for a given finer grained information entity. The other aspect of the information model will be to identify the entities' subset and their attribute subset that constitutes the information integration model at the given focus level. Just as when you connect an amplifier and a CD player, you don't care about the way the internal electronics are wired in each device, but you care about what is exposed by the connectors; similarly, the integration information model addresses the small entity subset that is required for integrating the various business components.

Efficient Enterprise Information Integration (EII) has often recommended the use of a canonical information model. Our approach here derives from the same principles but also looks at reducing the effort of designing and evolving such model by using some entity layer in the model and keeping the entity approach rather than unstructured attributes grouped in messages.

More detailed aspects of information integration that make it flexible, such as transience versus persistence or direct versus indirect relationships, are addressed in Chapter 3, "Implementing Dynamic Enterprise Information."

Enterprise Architecture Staged Zooming

As we saw in Chapter 1, the enterprise business is decomposed in several levels. Examples of that come from APQC, the BPMN standard, and IBM's Component Business Modeling (CBM) approach. The Process Classification Framework (PCF) from APQC[5] defines four levels: Categories, Process Groups, Processes, and Activities.

As discussed in Chapter 1, the BPMN defines three process categories: collaboration processes, abstract processes, and private processes. Even though it is subject to interpretation, in the following discussion, we use collaboration processes to describe exchanges with independent organizations, abstract processes for describing across lines of business in an enterprise or within different business rules owners in a given line of business, and private processes for what happens in the control of a single business owner.

IBM uses a two-level categorization in its CBM approach:

- **Business competencies**—Large business areas with related skills and capabilities, for example, new product development or financial management (these are equivalent to APQC categories or BPMN abstract processes). These business areas have multiple owners in the organization with different business goals, structured in various organizations.

- **Business component**—Acts as a service center that has the potential to operate independently. A business component occurs once only within the enterprise and delivers value to the enterprise through its ability to deliver a unique set of services implemented as processes that are potentially BPMN private processes if they have a single business owner. Many services are delivered in collaboration with other components both inside and outside the enterprise. Business component implementations may be multiple—for example, a provisioning component with two implementations, one for fixed line and one for mobile.

  However, each implementation of a business component has an identified owner in the organization. This is essential as business processes need explicit owners in the organization to be successful.

The participant, business owner, and actor roles are essential to structure the enterprise and business processes for dynamicity and agility. So, how are these roles defined?

A participant is the organization from which the business viewpoint is constructed. It can be a line of business, a department, or a business component as the boundary of an organization.

A business owner is the party that defines the business rules and policies of a given subset of tasks and business processes. Depending on enterprise governance structure, this could be a physical person or a team. But in the majority of cases, there are multiple owners for different aspects of the business in the enterprise. A dynamic enterprise usually lets each owner optimize his domain of responsibility within the constraints of external contracts.

An actor is any human or technical entity that contributes and interacts with the business component or process.

Even though actors and participants may be identified, the BPMN, XPDL, or WS-BPEL specifications do not give any guidance about business ownership. In my experience, multiple ownership of a single business process leads to long-term manageability issues and lowers the value of the process. This is why a practical method needs to consider this ownership to define the manageability boundaries of explicit private processes. This does not imply that end-to-end processes do not exist, but rather that the realization is modular because there are business contracts between areas controlled by different business owners. The interchange between two different owners is a contract, expressed as a business service. Identifying such contracts is an integral part of the decomposition.

The staged zooming approach as represented in Figure 2-5 consists of a focused decomposition at each level, based on a combination of the previously mentioned processes and pattern categorizations extracting only the elements needed at that given level. The elements include services, processes, information, and policies. The analysis also includes context, contract, and content identification with variability evaluation based on requirements.

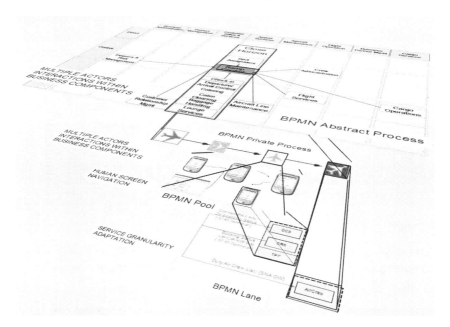

Figure 2-5 Zooming the typical layers of interaction

Let me reinforce the necessity of separating the process layers and particularly the abstract activity flows from executable design with this quote:

> One goal of XPDL 2.1 is to promote portability of abstract activity flow models between tools. This requires separating the elements and attributes of BPMN related to activity flow modeling from those related to executable design.[6]

Robert M. Shapiro, Vice Chair, WfMC Technical Committee

In our method, we apply a more detailed categorical analysis on executable designs, where the analysis is complemented with a pattern approach that structures the implementation toward the use of best fit standard-based technologies for each pattern. Mixing patterns, such as the enterprise process driving multiple actors with a single user driving a local process, in a BPM implementation is a common pitfall that leads to lack of reusability and manageability.

The practical method starts by identifying the appropriate stereotypes at each level of the identified focus elements, and then variation is applied at the same level. Then, we zoom to the next level focus elements, and so on until services and pools or lanes are reached. Figure 2-6 shows these stereotypes applied to a UML model in Rational® Software Architect.

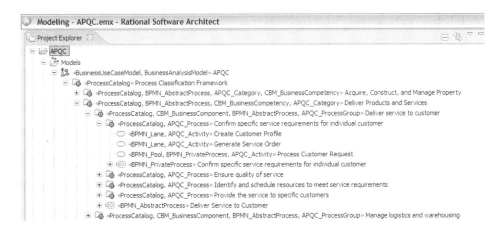

Figure 2-6   Capturing APQC, BPMN, and CBM stereotypes in UML models

By applying these stereotypes and implementation patterns with variability, we ensure both the required process dynamicity and the most effective implementation using selected technical standards. This approach allows these standards to provide an acceleration of the development cycle and maintenance aspects. The patterns that foster a manageable separation of process aspects are described in the following chapters.

Dynamic Patterns for Staged Decomposition

Architecture is really about the separation of concerns. Different concerns lead to different patterns. Thus, mixing patterns in process design often leads to the use of inappropriate technical standards in the implementation. It is essential to identify the patterns that help the staged decomposition provide flexibility. Here are two patterns we use in further discussion:

- **Enterprise push pattern**—This first pattern applies to the first levels of enterprise business decomposition, where the enterprise owns and drives the sequencing of steps and pushes events or service calls to the various enterprise actors, business components, or business services. These can be BPMN abstract processes, private processes, or even pools with multiple lanes if multiple actors are involved. Subsequent decomposition of this pattern is based on business ownership.

- **Single actor pull pattern**—Farther down, at the levels including tasks and services, is where a single actor as the consumer of the services is integrated. The actor is either a person in a given role, or a programmatic service consumer that gets to enterprise resources and applications. The actor is the principal driver of the next step of the flow. This pattern is equivalent to a BPMN lane as a lane is constructed from an actor's point of view. Subsequent decomposition of this pattern is based on purpose and technical nature of the actor.

Enterprise Push Pattern Levels

To model the enterprise push levels with appropriate flexibility, we have to refine the pattern in two stages with specific operating conditions. This also helps in selecting and applying the correct technical standards for improved manageability.

It is essential to identify the ownership of the rules that govern the sequence of tasks or services. For further decomposition of business components, it is also necessary to materialize the effective boundaries between lines of business and within a line of business.

The main pattern differentiation here is based on business ownership. We need to layer the interactions that involve multiple business owners leading to BPMN abstract processes, dissecting the subset of processes, rules, and core entities in control of a single business owner involving multiple actors and resulting in BPMN private processes.

Interactions Between Lines of Business or Business Components

At this stage, we zoom in on the interactions between lines of business or business components that should only include business sequence allowing top-level interactions based on business contracts. These contracts are materialized as events or requests/replies with neither loops nor decisions. This layer structures the work split between enterprise entities, but these interactions are driven from within the business components where the logic resides.

This level is what BPMN categorizes as abstract processes, because the end-to-end process behavior is implicitly realized by the chaining of explicit choreographies using either services calls or events.

At this level, the business analyst, architect, and modeler need to

- Capture business requirements external to the focus business component.

- Analyze context, contract, and content variations and formalize them with taxonomies.

- Establish enterprise contribution of each business component, or single owner process groups, to the value chain with enterprise level Key Performance Indicators (KPIs).

- Analyze enterprise level service level agreements and their measurements.

- Establish a high-level core entity information model that the focus domain needs in its interactions, with a distance-based analysis of information attribute details.

- Materialize the interaction information based on the core entity model.

- Derive enterprise level business sequences from business interactions.

- Define business rules owners on the selected focus business domain, that is, who owns what business sequence in a given business component.

- Define major enterprise actors on the selected focus business domain. These actors can be different from owners.

- Finalize starting and ending business events.

Figure 2-7 shows a presales enterprise level process, flowing through several business participant organizations, which are customer relationship management, telecommunication service management, resource management, and supplier/partner management. Each organization operates independently and exposes interactions based on contracts using the top-level information model entities, such as Product and Product Order.

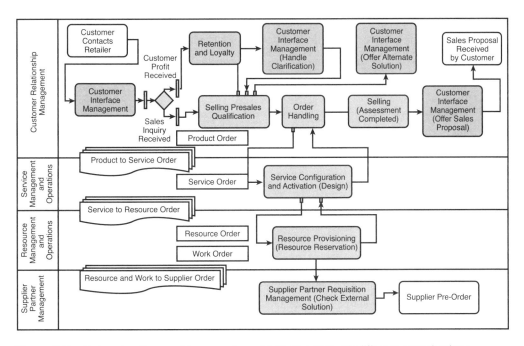

Figure 2-7   Enterprise flow pushing events and activities through different organizations

At the enterprise level, the business process is realized by each organization's implicit or explicit management, but this process is what business management of the enterprise needs to monitor. The KPIs identified at that level are the cross organization enterprise indicators to be monitored. It is in no way a monitoring of a workflow automation engine, but a monitoring model based on the high-level implicit process with essential views of the enterprise business dynamics. In addition, even though this monitoring model can be created from process modeling tools, it is not expected to be implemented as an explicit workflow in a workflow or BPEL engine.

The common standards for the processes at this level are BPMN representation. Using XPDL interchange format for the models may be a problem as the XPDL metamodel does not support packages within packages, and thus cannot be used to capture models such as APQC or eTOM.

On the contrary, UML activity diagrams and XML Metadata Interchange (XMI) allow package trees, as well as proprietary interchange format such as IBM WebSphere® Business Modeler XML format.[7]

Technical standards for this level also include information related models, with Web Ontology Language (OWL) for ontology, XML schemas, or Service Data Objects (SDOs) with the variability to define events and abstracted messaging standards for the transport of the interactions.

Multiple Actor Interactions within Single Owner Business Components

At this level, we zoom in on the interactions with a business component and the workflows between actors.

This stage targets the modeling of the explicit behavior of the business component and the "to-be" business processes. It includes defining the business decisions and loop details for relevant business processes in a process group, and the identification of business services exposing these process models as well as the business services and the operation consumed by these processes.

At this stage, the business analyst, architect, and modeler need to capture the following in formal models:

- Understand the completeness of the workflow within a business component and its use of external interactions as identified in the previous stage.

- Define the business rules and policies that govern that business component or process group, with alternate flows and business exceptions.

- Understand the business behavior of the underlying technical implementation realization. As all enterprises have existing applications, these applications need to be analyzed from a business perspective for completeness and variation analysis.

- Establish the multiactor workflow process decision structure and detail the multiactor sequence accordingly. The modeling focuses on enterprise push and thus needs to explicitly exclude sequences of tasks operated by a single actor acting as a consumer pulling from the system the next action (such as screen navigation or transient sequences in threads). These single-actor-centered sequences should be grouped in a higher level construct business task.

- Define the actors' roles and groups when these actors are humans.

- Define the business component level KPIs that will be the result of the operations of the explicit business processes at this level.

The technical standards for this level are workflow and services choreography standards: WS-BPEL, BPEL4People,[8] and the WS-HumanTask specification. It is essential to differentiate the exposure to a private process of a human task exposed as service that looks at generic human roles and people assignments of tasks and the implementation of the same task that looks at the actions from that given person in that role on the specific tasks.

In Figure 2-8, extracted from the BPEL4People specification, many people qualify as voters for the employee of the month. Each individual voting for the employee probably has a sequence of screens that are part of the Elect Employee of the Month task, such as review achievements and look at personal history, but all of these are considered as being of a lower level and part of the Human task.

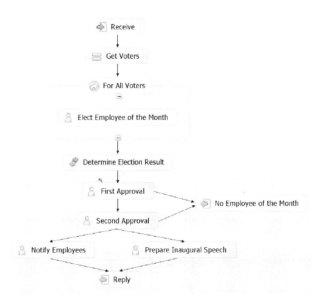

Figure 2-8   BPEL4People standard sample process

The process described previously is a private process occurring in a business component, possibly a CBM store operations management or human resource management component.

As the BPEL4People source in Figure 2-9 shows, the task =`"approveEmployeeOfTheMonth"` is associated with a Web Service operation and portType, which is pushed to the defined logicalPeopleGroup.

```
<htd:tasks>

            <htd:task name="approveEmployeeOfTheMonth">

                <htd:documentation xml:lang="en-US">

                        The reusable definition of the task
                        used to approve the election of the
                        employee of the month.

                </htd:documentation>

            <htd:interface operation="approve"
            portType="hr:approvalPT"/>

            <htd:peopleAssignments>

                <htd:potentialOwners>

                    <htd:from
                    logicalPeopleGroup="approvers">

                    <!-- variables used here need to be
                    defined on the enclosing scope or
                    above -->

                        <htd:argument name="region">

                            $electionRequest/region

                        </htd:argument>

                    </htd:from>

                </htd:potentialOwners>

            </htd:peopleAssignments>

            <htd:presentationElements/>1

            </htd:task>

    </htd:tasks>
```

Figure 2-9   BPEL4People source sample

Even though the standard defines presentationElements[9] the process designer must be careful to separate what describes the dynamics of an end user screen interaction in a separate layer. BPEL4People was never intended to describe GUI flows and event handling.

Single Actor Pull Pattern Levels

If we look at the **single actor pull pattern** modeling level, we have to refine the pattern in two single actor sub patterns:

- **Human screen navigation task**—An example of these interactions can be a person in a call center selling a product to a customer on the phone and a teller in a bank performing a money withdrawal or any low-grained task.

- **Granularity and semantic adaptation**—This level consists of computer-based short running flows, mostly used to handle service granularity adaptation from existing services or APIs as provided by existing applications or partners and an isolation layer of reusable business service operations implementing flexibility. This layer also applies routing and dynamic binding based on context, contract, and content.

Human Screen Navigation

At lower levels, usually the fourth level of APQC, the tasks are delivered by a human as complex interactions from a single actor with a user interface. The need for extracting these sequences globally qualified as a human task comes from the specific nonfunctional requirements of such interactions. For example, a customer calling a call center to buy car insurance can interact with a call center operator on the phone during several minutes to capture contract conditions, but at any step of this discussion may want to go back to a previous step to change parameters or options. This type of sequence is potentially highly interactive and requires extensive event support as well as user friendliness. It is not a simple flow of application services or linear sequence of screens.

In addition, the isolation of such global task modeling in a different stage allows the handling of multiple channels as variations of this global human task implementation dynamically linked at runtime based on other conditions or policies. Such dynamic selection is exposed in Chapter 6, "Implementing the Enterprise Expansion Joint."

Several technical standards exist, such as Java™ Server Faces (JSF) or Struts for handling dynamic screen navigation, AJAX for local HTML page GUI dynamics, or Eclipse for Rich clients. The advantage of JSF is its server-side navigation rule definition in XML files that allows changing screen navigation without modifying code and provides a better security. As shown in Figure 2-10, these navigation rules are easy to interpret.

```
<navigation-rule>
    <from-view-id>/logon.jsp</from-view-id>
    <navigation-case>
        <from-outcome>logon_success</from-outcome>
        <to-view-id>/contents.jsp</to-view-id>
        <redirect/>
    </navigation-case>
    <navigation-case>
        <from-outcome>logon_failure</from-outcome>
        <to-view-id>/logon.jsp</to-view-id>
    </navigation-case>
<navigation-rule>
```

Figure 2-10   Sample JSF navigation rule

One additional concern at this layer is the handling of information, both contextual and persistent, and specific to the end user client GUI application life cycle.

It is not expected that all the data exposed to a person will flow through private processes. A principle for making processes flexible is that only information that is required for process decisions should be carried through the process. Other information attributes should be accessed using a layer of Information as a Service (IaaS) built from analysis of the information model and the persistence as expected from a Master Data Management implementation.

As an example, Figure 2-11 shows a typical structured context hierarchy that some banks apply for their branches. The same core entity may be present in the various contexts and the client GUI applications. Look for a given entity identified by a key starting with the lower context and then navigating up the tree. The number of levels in the tree varies, and in Figure 2-11, the

lower level allows the branch officer to handle multiple customer interactions, such as one requiring immediate attention at the front desk, while treating other background tasks that do no require
immediate attention such as handling banking by mail. If the data is not existent in any context, it
can be preserved in the context by caching information retrieved from using an IaaS. A common
example is to retrieve all of a given customer's accounts at the first interaction and cache them in
the local context to speed up the following operations and reduce the number of interactions with
central sites.

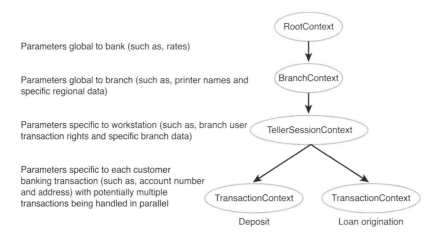

Figure 2-11   Typical banking teller operations context structure

Of course, such information caching needs to comply with appropriate security requirements and may require additional signing and encryption to prevent unauthorized access.

Granularity Adaptation

The last element in the single actor pull pattern is a programmatic actor in charge of exposing the
appropriate granularity of services. As we saw in Chapter 1 in the discussion of service operations, granularity that has reusability value for the enterprise is usually at a level 4 or level 5 of
decomposition.

The idea behind flexibility is to make the new processes and client application as independent from the existing implementation as possible by using a layer of service that derives from a
decomposition analysis and is kept at a coarse interface level. However, the existing applications,
APIs, functions, or services usually have a lower granularity and need to be aggregated to be
exposed with the appropriate granularity and variability of the interface.

It follows that there is a need for a matchmaking layer that exposes the flexible and variable
granularity on one side and performs the required adaptation to existing lower granularities.
Pushing this adaptation to the lower layers and as close as possible to the target implementation

also tremendously simplifies the handling of nonfunctional requirements, such as consistency with units of work, security adaptation, and reliability.

Many techniques exist to realize this granularity adaptation, such as fan out and fan in, microflows in BPEL, split information model with or without information context buffering, semantic adaptation, and so on. All these techniques are discussed in Chapter 6.

Summary

The base of an architectural approach is the separation of concerns and a good identification of context and requirements. In this chapter, we saw a focused approach that examines combining a pragmatic horizon-based technique to limit the effort while zooming down the appropriate pattern levels.

Requirement changes deriving from business or technical changes always occur in the enterprise. This approach seeks to limit the propagation of a change, by defining a succession of layers, creating borders that have the potential of containing the changes within their boundaries, or enabling the change to be managed by the variability that occurs between the layers.

Processes are similar to mechanical engines in that they require the variability and standardization of both semantics and technical interfaces. Without this realization, we face the issues of limited reusability. In the following chapters, we discuss variability and flexibility of implementation techniques, based on concrete experiences.

CHAPTER 3

Implementing Dynamic Enterprise Information

The most important thing that was new was the idea of URI or URL, that any piece of information anywhere should have an identifier, which will allow you to get hold of it.

Tim Berners-Lee

A World of Dynamic and Variable Information

Why dynamic and variable information? Taking an example information domain, any industry product catalog usually has monthly, if not shorter, evolutions. More than 300,000 trademark applications[1] have been filed in the United States.[2] Given the number of manufacturing businesses in the United States, this equates to more than one trademark per year per enterprise, often with each trademark covering more than one product in a catalog. For example, IBM issued around 140 announcement letters in December 2008.[3]

These catalog changes or product additions or deletions are reflected as information changes and may induce a different type of characteristics structure. The telecommunications industry offers a basic example of evolution with the convergence of media and telecommunication channels. We can expect to see bundles of mobile phone services that include broadband and media services. For example, with the same product subscription you might be able to begin watching a sports match or any on-demand show on mobile phone TV while away from home, and then switch to IP or cable television at home all included in the same bundle.

Even though coping with information changes is business as usual in the IT world, we strive to limit the impact of an information change, particularly if that information is carried by service interfaces and handled in business processes across the enterprise. If an enterprise has an integrated order management process, it is difficult, even impossible sometimes, to have catalog changes require an end-to-end process test, just because that information modification induced an XML schema change.

The U.S. Federal Enterprise Architecture Data Reference Model (DRM) explicitly separates data model, data context, and data sharing. Quoting from the DRM document: "The need for data sharing often manifests itself in ways that are difficult to predict in advance."[4]

Before we look at techniques for implementing the variability needed on data sharing, as any information exposed by a service can be qualified, we need to find a workable trade-off between fully variable information, such as unstructured documents, and fully rigid information models where an entity variation requires a new class of objects with strongly typed attributes.

Delimiting the Variability

As introduced in Chapter 2, "Streamlining the Enterprise Architecture for Dynamic BPM and SOA," an information domain decomposition analysis is necessary to find the stable information elements and their variation space. Classical data modeling methods or standards, such as the (ISO/IEC) 11179 Metadata Registries standard, do not explicitly address variability, but rather address it indirectly using classifications, conceptual or value domains, and nonenumerated domains defined by the information content by description. We want not only to define the classifications, but also to identify manageable extensibility points of classifications. The usual content approaches for information modeling are complemented with contextual and contractual business capabilities, an identification of both context evolutions and contractual evolutions between information stakeholders.

The resulting approach has two dimensions: The first dimension is the architectural life cycle and phase, and the second dimension covers the aspects of the information model that structures the variation identification. The phases start with the business requirements, business capabilities, and use cases. The next step is the identification of the information elements implied by the requirements and use cases. The last phase is the specification of the information elements and data.

The information architect analyzes contextual aspects from a business context or environment first, then looks at the information life cycle context, and finally examines the technical context specification to formalize information sources and variability requirements. Then the content looks at grouping classifications with a shared and consensual terminology, used for information sharing and exchange, respectively called taxonomy and ontology.

- **Taxonomy** refers to a system of hierarchical types that can be used to describe entities. The types are expressed in a class and subclass system. In our case, the taxonomy hierarchy is the base for the domain decomposition.

- **Ontology** refers to a description of things that exist, their properties and their relationships to each other. It defines the various elements that can be used to describe and represent a domain of knowledge. The ontology includes definitions of basic concepts within a domain or across domains and the relationships among them using the elements, such as classes, individuals, and properties.

Taxonomies and ontologies structure the information with stable groups, which can then be shared within a **community of interest**. Finally, the contract aspect looks at the sharing aspects and the dynamics of that sharing. This aspect examines the business and technical information exchange packages that are required to fulfill the business capabilities. The exchange packages are always views of core entities that are managed by participants in a community of interest. The contractual aspects need to clarify the sharing requirements and use the contextual information to capture the various implications of the contract. Table 3-1, derived from the previously mentioned Federal Data Reference model, summarizes the approach activities.

Table 3-1   Information Architecture Aspects

		Context	Content (Identification and Description)	Contract (Sharing)
Information Architecture Phase	Business conceptualization	What are the core entities and subentities needed to support the business and mission needs and its evolutions? Map the entities onto a business component map, competencies, and communities of interest. Decompose into levels to identify subentities.	From the context and usage define the ontologies and taxonomies that will convey the information. Identify appropriate industry domain-specific standards (OAGIS, SID, CIM, IEC 61970). Define taxonomy and variability principles.	Define information sharing patterns and establish the service level agreements for these patterns. Establish information consumer provider matrixes and potential evolutions. Establish nonfunctional requirements.
	Specification	Define ownership of subject areas and entities of interest. Specify information governance principles, processes, policies, and stakeholders. Specify core information that the makes the data discoverable and establish governance.	Define the abstract data model, specify stable subject areas and subentities. From context and use case variation analysis, specify variability patterns, including child entities, entity relationships, and attributes.	Specify the service catalog required to support the data sharing needs of the various participants' enterprise community of interest or line of business.

Table 3-1   Information Architecture Aspects

		Context	Content (Identi-fication and Description)	Contract (Sharing)
	Implementa-tion	Identify data sources and stewardship. Define roles. Define an architectural abstract information layering that isolates the model from data sources and specify the connection approaches for integrating new sources and categories of sources.	Specify logical model and variability patterns (see following chapters for pattern specification). Implement the ontologies.	Specify services in the catalog, using payload specification that conforms to the specification of the variability patterns. Verify the granularity of information services by mapping the services on a functional decomposition.

Business Analysis

The business analysis information modeling part looks at relating business goals and requirements to a set of core entities, content, and sharing identification.

Core Entity Identification and Business Mapping

In this section, we find to answer the "what:" What does the enterprise manage, and who creates and is the primary owner of the "what?" Working through examples helps clarify the high-level conceptual issues. One question the enterprise business may raise is do we consider any actor that interacts with the enterprise management to be an involved party, or do we consider that a customer has as specific domain by itself, with a specific information domain attached to that entity.

IBM's Financial Service Data Model (shown in Table 3-2) represents the business information requirements of a generic financial services organization, along with the necessary rules to ensure information integrity. It represents the business information needs and requirements of the financial services organization using common terms that are understood by business professionals and identifies nine high-level classes called **Data Concepts**.

Table 3-2 IBM's Financial Service Data Model[5]

Concept or Domain	Description
Involved Party	Represents all participants that may have contact with the financial services organization or that are of interest to the financial services organization and about which the financial services organization wants to maintain information. This includes information about the financial services organization itself. Customers are considered as implicitly part of the Involved Party domain.
Product	Describes goods and services that can be offered, sold, or purchased by the financial services organization, its competitors, and other involved parties during the normal course of business. The data concept also includes nonfinancial goods and services that are of interest to the financial services organization.
Arrangement	Represents a potential or actual agreement between two or more involved parties (individuals, organizations, or organizational units) related to a product, which provides and affirms the rules and obligations associated with the sale, exchange, or provision of goods, services, or resources.
Business Direction Item	Records an expression of an involved party's intent with regard to the manner and environments in which it wants to carry out its business.
Condition	Describes the specific requirements that relate to how the business of a financial services organization is conducted and includes information such as prerequisite or qualification criteria and restrictions or limits associated with these requirements. Conditions can apply to any aspects of a financial services organization's operations.
Classification	Organizes and manages business information by defining a taxonomy structure that provides classification categories that apply to one or more concepts.
Event	Describes a happening about which the financial services organization wants to keep information as a part of carrying out its mission and conducting its business.
Location	Describes a place where something can be found, a destination of information or a bounded area, such as a country or state, about which the financial services organization wants to keep information.
Resource Item	Includes and describes any value item, either tangible or intangible, that is owned, managed, used by, or of specific interest to the financial services organization in pursuit and accomplishment of its business.

The telecommunication operators have a slightly different view of the core domains and differentiate the base entities from the enterprise and the specific business domains for each entity, as shown in Table 3-3.

Table 3-3   TeleManagement Forum Telecommunication Industry Shared Information and Data (SID) Model Standard's Data Concepts

Concept or Domain	Description
Customer Domain	Includes all data and contract operations associated with individuals or organizations that obtain products from an enterprise, such as a service provider. It represents all types of contact with the customer, the management of the relationship, and the administration of customer data. As a notable difference from the financial model, the customer is considered a separate information domain even though technically the SID Unified Modeling Language (UML) model makes the customer entity derive from a common party entity. But as described, this domain includes much more information than simply the customer entity, such as the contracts related to that customer that would be in the Arrangement domain in Table 3-2.
Supplier/Partner	Not only defines the supplier or partner "party" but also includes all supplier and partner-oriented data and contract operations. This is again a difference from the financial model previously described in Table 3-2, which would consider the Supplier/Partner as an Involved Party and its contracts as Arrangements.
Market/Sales Domain	Includes the information about data and contract operations that support the sales and marketing activities needed to gain business from customers and potential customers.
Product Domain	Is concerned with the life cycle of products and information and contract operations related to products' life cycle. It contains entities that deal with the strategic portfolio plans, products offered, product performance, product usage statistics, as well as the product instances delivered to a customer.
Service Domain	Contains the definition, development, and operational aspects of services provided and managed by a telecommunication operator, including service level agreement, deployment and configuration, and management of problems in a service life cycle.
Resource Domain	Consists of the information related to definition, development, and operational aspects of the information computing and processing infrastructure of a telecommunication operator system, including logical resources such as an e-mail address or physical resources such as a set top box.
Common Business Entities Domain	Contains the entities shared across two or more other domains. An example is Party as it is shared between customer and Supplier/Partner and is not "owned" by any particular domain. In some cases a common business entity represents a generic abstraction of other real-world business entities.

Looking at Figure 3-1, which compares the TeleManagement SID party model with IBM's IFW financial information framework, we can see that the customer deriving from Party in the TMF SID model and the Involved Party in the IBM model are closely related at the top level.

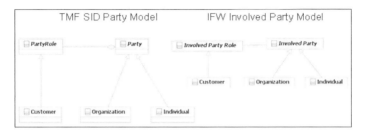

Figure 3-1   Comparison of SID and IFW party models

So why does the TeleManagement Forum SID standard separate the Customer domain as a separate model? The reasoning behind this separation is the possibility of many more party roles in a telecommunication operator environment. In this environment, the specific "customer" role can be far more complex.

With the convergence of the telco and media industries, we can expect a lot of variability in the nature of parties involved in a telco business, and the information model needs to allow for this variability. In their new business models, telecommunication operators are getting less revenue from the connection itself and have to rely on content such as streaming video and gaming, which is often owned and controlled by other parties. They also look at valuing the information that they know from their customers, such as presence and location, to provide value added services that also link to function or process providers for applications.

An example of this type of model is fleet management, where knowing the exact location of the transportation may help with additional business. This is reflected in the SID party model where vendors, functions or process providers, intermediaries, and additional roles that may be needed are defined. Defining these parties as information classes has value only if the business model requires managing information for each of these parties.

Figure 3-2 is an excerpt of the SID model that shows the variability we're discussing.

As you may already have anticipated from the diagrams in Figures 3-1 and 3-2, UML is a convenient way to capture the decompositions in a formal way. The domain decomposition can be represented as a package tree in UML but also as catalog trees in other tools.

Figure 3-3 shows a UML view of the standard SID model in Rational Software Architect, as made available in the Rational model from the TeleManagement Forum site.[6] These figures show an expansion of the Product Offering Aggregate Business Entities (ABE) together with the same representation of the information domains in a WebSphere Business Modeler process modeling tool. The package tree from the UML is semantically equivalent to a business item catalog structure in the process modeling tool. The business items are equivalent to classes or XML simple or complex types.

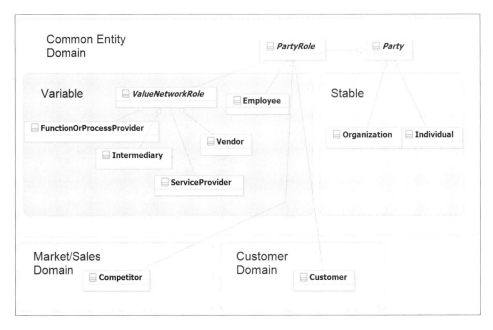

Figure 3-2   Variability of party roles in the SID model

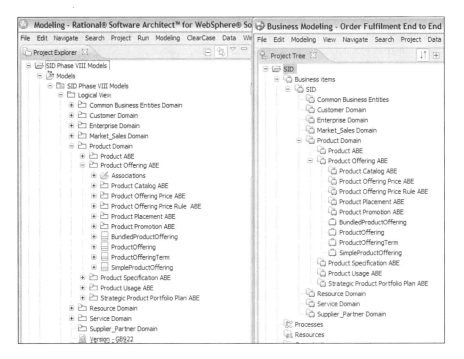

Figure 3-3   Representation of domain decomposition in UML and process modeling tools

As modeling tools include transformations and various import and export features, it is important to ensure the consistency of the representation of the domain structures across models and artifacts.

Similarly, when XML schemas are used to represent the enterprise information, the domain decomposition structure is translated into namespaces declarations, as shown in Figure 3-4.

http://www.ibm.com/soabpm/SID/CustomerDomain
http://www.ibm.com/soabpm/SID/EnterpriseDomain
http://www.ibm.com/soabpm/SID/MarketSalesDomain
http://www.ibm.com/soabpm/SID/ProductDomain
http://www.ibm.com/soabpm/SID/ProductDomain/ProductABE
http://www.ibm.com/soabpm/SID/ProductDomain/ProductOfferingABE
http://www.ibm.com/soabpm/SID/ProductDomain/ProductOfferingABE/ProductCatalogABE
http://www.ibm.com/soabpm/SID/ProductDomain/ProductOfferingABE/ProductOfferingPriceABE

Figure 3-4 Representation of data model structures as namespaces

Now that the business information domains are identified, business classifications can be created for the content of each of these domains.

Definition of Ontologies and Taxonomies

Taxonomies are classifications of things that exist. The use of a classification is essential for an enterprise to lift ambiguities in the business operation. These classifications are, however, often implicit, and it is essential that one understand that the basis for consistent business rules definition requires a formalization of this classification. Taxonomy is not a new concept, and often companies employ a data dictionary, which is an equivalent concept.

For example, IBM has an internally created taxonomy that relates to its business domains and its business data standards. Table 3-4 is a small extract of this taxonomy that is general enough to be in public domain but shows some of the business terms that relate to the integrated supply chain and the distribution information domain (referred to here as Business Data Standard).

This taxonomy is a good starting point, but as it is just a table in a document or a Web page, there is still a missing link if we are to use this taxonomy in a computer-driven formal model way.

This taxonomy model formalization can be delivered using the W3C RDF Vocabulary Description Language standard.[7] This **Resource Description Framework (RDF)** is initially a general-purpose language for the Web; however, it has the necessary constructs for capturing taxonomies in XML. RDF defines XML statements that link subjects to values or objects with classification elements of the taxonomy (predicates). In addition, RDF defines **label** as the human-readable property of resources. Table 3-4 contains many such terms.

Suppose we have an input message that carries an order with a product name. We can apply a transformation to generate an RDF document compatible with the enterprise taxonomy from the input message. Then in the resulting RDF document, the predicate ProductName with the label Product Name from the taxonomy links the object InputMessage with a resource value as a URI, defining how the product name is identified in the message. WebSphere Business Services Fabric has a different approach, in which the RDF document is built from a context injector written in Java in the service components. In addition, if policies and rules are required, there will be a need for more complex relations between classes, cardinality (for example, exactly one), equality, richer typing of properties, characteristics of properties (for example, symmetry), and enumerated classes.

Table 3-4   Sample Taxonomy Elements

Nr.	Taxonomy Term	Data Steward	Date Created	Business Area	Business Data Standard
267	Ship Weight Rate Code	Janet Doe	15/11/2004	Integrated Supply Chain	Distribution
268	Shipping Material Group	John Doe	15/11/2004	Integrated Supply Chain	Distribution
269	Storage Class	Janet Doe	15/11/2004	Integrated Supply Chain	Distribution
270	Transportatio n Group	John Doe	21/10/2004	Integrated Supply Chain	Distribution

Ontology provides one way of encoding a model and has been adopted as one layer in the semantic Web. The ontology usually includes such concepts in the domain of interest, relationships among them, their properties, and their values. One use of ontology is to externalize a model and make it easier for business applications to share and/or reuse knowledge and improve information navigation and search by using reasoning. Furthermore, the externalization of models facilitates customization of an application without modifying code. The support provided by the Web Ontology Language (OWL) builds on RDF and extends the notions of classes, relationships, and content.

The creation of RDFs and OWLs is facilitated by profiles in UML tooling. Figure 3-5 provides an example of a UML diagram that represents OWL classes and RDF notations and can be transformed directly to OWL files using a Rational model transformation.[8]

Business Information Sharing

The business information sharing requirements between business domains and components derive from the business capabilities and requirements. At this stage, we look at identifying the high life cycle of the information core entities within a business map. In the majority of cases, the information sharing requirements dictate whether to provide initial details or update the state across the interactions on the core entities. Again, in the majority of cases, there is a core entity in the center of an exchange or a business process. An order to cash process is centered on a customer order and its avatars, similarly, service assurance processes look at trouble tickets, and case management is defined by case core entity.

Figure 3-5   Example of OWL classes and RDF elements in UML

A representation of information circulation is the basis for this identification. In Figure 3-6, we use the a subset of the eTOM business decomposition map in the operation domains to show a high-level flow of an order to cash interaction and the sharing requirements represented as entities.

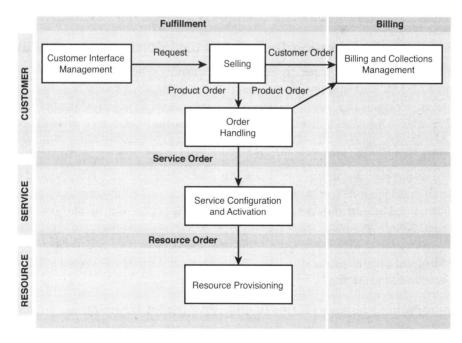

Figure 3-6   Positioning exchange entities on business maps

These entities are Request or the unspecified initial customer interaction; Customer Order, which would be the result of an interaction in a commercial order; Product Order or the specific instantiation of a product for a customer; Service Order, which includes the services that must be configured for the product to be delivered; and Resource Order, or the resources that need to be provisioned for the services to be operational.

The sharing entities are exchange payload packages as identified by the Federal Data Reference model. These sharing entities carry views or references of the core entities managed by each business component.

Another way of locating shared information is to create consumer/provider matrixes that have business components as both line and column headers, and define the sharing entities. Applying the same order as shown in Figure 3-6 for a cash example brings us to the example of a consumer provider matrix and the shared information entities. However, as you can see in Figure 3-7, large business map matrixes have the potential to grow too much to be conveniently handled this way. In such a case, the simplified map with overlays in Figure 3-6 appears more convenient.

Another deduction from the matrix representation in Figure 3-7 is that there could be many different information sharing entities with potential interactions between any of an enterprise business map. As a result, if we look at making the enterprise integration more flexible we have to limit these entities by making them more general. The total number of information sharing packages would definitely be limited by introducing flexibility in the shared information. In Figure 3-7, we use the same Product Order to carry the request and the replies, implying that the status structures are embedded inside that entity.

Simple Implementation Techniques for Information Variability

There are some basic techniques for introducing variability in the implementation of information. As the same logical information may have several physical representations, we list here the essential variations that can be represented in any language (primarily Java and XML). This information in messages is often referred to as **data sharing** or **exchange payload**.

Using "Any," "Object," or "Void *"

Often sharing payloads have a common stable header and may carry a varying payload that is of no interest to the integration or mediation layers. There is a need to represent that payload so that it can be carried between provider and consumer, allowing both ends to decide how to interpret the content. In XML, this is defined as **xsd:any type**; in Java, it's an **Object**; and in C it's a **void ***.

As shown in Figure 3-8, Open Applications Group Interface Specification (OAGIS) is a standard that uses this xsd:any to define the userArea. It is used as an extension for all business objects defined in the standard.

Name/Value Pairs and Name/Value Type Triplet Techniques

The "any" approach is good for varying payloads, but we may still need to allow the mediation layers to identify some of the elements that are carried.

From	To	Customer Relationship Management: Customer Interface Management	Customer Relationship Management: Selling	Customer Relationship Management: Order Handling	Customer Relationship Management: Billing and Collections Management	Service Management and Operations: Service Configuration and Activation	Resource Management and Operations: Resource Provisioning
Customer Relationship Management	Customer Interface Management		Request				
Customer Relationship Management	Selling	Request Confirm		Product Order	Customer Order	Selling	
Service Management of Operations	Order Handling		Product Order (Confirm)		Product Order (Completed)	Service Order	Order Handling
Service Management of Operations	Service Configuration and Activation			Service Order (Activation Notification Status)			Resource Order
Resource Management and Operations	Resource Provisioning					Resource Order (Provisioning Complete Status Notification)	

Figure 3-7 Consumer provider business information sharing matrix

XML view:

```
<xsd:complexType name="UserAreaType">
 <xsd:sequence>
    <xsd:any namespace="##any" processContents="strict" minOccurs="0"
maxOccurs="unbounded"/>
</xsd:sequence>
</xsd:complexType>
```

UML® view:

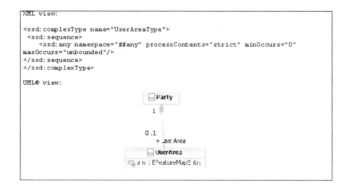

Figure 3-8 User area extension in OAGIS

Simple Single Pair Approaches

In a project we delivered with a large German IT provider, there was a request to provide varying information queries. To achieve that, we created a wish list based on arrays of simple name/value pairs. By using this technique, we were able to handle the varying requests of this IT provider from different clients, each requiring a different set of values for the same core entities (such as account, product, or party).

Using name/value pairs accelerates the interpretation of the values simply because both ends have knowledge of what the "name" is and can easily morph these constructs in hash tables for quick access. Even though the value could be anything (as with xsd:any in the previous section), in most cases, it is defined as a string representation of the value, such as in Figure 3-9.

```
<xsd:complexType name="nameValuePair">
      <xsd:sequence>
        <xsd:element name="elementName" type="String">    </xsd:element>
        <xsd:element name="elementValue" type="String">    </xsd:element>
      </xsd:sequence>
</xsd:complexType>
<xsd:element name="wishList" type="nameValuePair" minOccurs="0"
maxOccurs="unbounded"/>
```

Figure 3-9   Typical name/value pair definition in an XML schema

The OAGIS standard also defines a name/value pair type that includes interpretation of types as shown in Figure 3-10, using unitCode to describe the string representation of the identified value content type.

Figure 3-10   UML representation of OAGIS NameValuePair XML type

However, these name/value pair constructs still leave the information extensibility as a flat array extension, and do not clearly separate the specification of the valued element from its value instantiation. When present the type is repeated in all instances, instead of defining it once. This leads us to a more structured method, as implemented by some other standards.

Structured Approaches (Telco SID Standard Approach)

The SID telco information model has a more versatile information variability approach. It extensively uses a characteristic specification and value pattern, where a characteristic of an entity has a specification with a name, type, description, and cardinality information, and is instantiated as a value that points to that specification. Each value can reference other sets of values, which in turn enables trees of valuation for characteristic specifications.

Even though SID uses that pattern in all domains, it does not refer to the base Characteristic-Value type in all its core entities, but rather specifies for some domains adding stable attributes to that set of characteristics, such as in the case of a core entity domain like Product Pricing influence.

In summary, the SID is a reference example of how the same CharacteristicValue variability pattern can be optimized for some well-known and less variable business entity attributes. Figure 3-11 shows the detailed UML model for CharacteristicValue and how it relates to either model based entities.

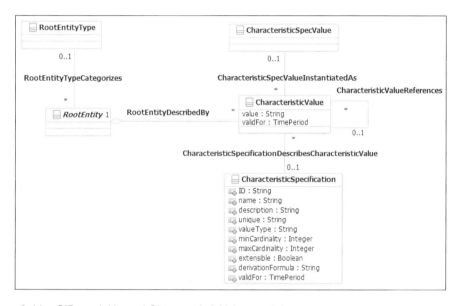

Figure 3-11   SID model based CharacteristicValue model

The value tree in Figure 3-12 shows an XML instantiation of the UML model shown in Figure 3-11.

```
<CustomerOrderMessage>
    <CustomerOrder      id="MyOrderIdentifier">
        <CharacteristicValue specId="BundleOrder" value="PHONE BUNDLE"/>
        <CharacteristicValue specId="requestedDeliveryDate"
                            value="01/01/2009"/>
        <ProductOrderItem id="PHONE_RENTAL">
            <CharacteristicValue specId="Feature"
                                value="CALL_WAITING" />
            <CharacteristicValue specId="Feature"
                                value="CALLER_DISPLAY"/>
            <CharacteristicValue specId="RingTone"
                                value="Classic Phone"/>
        </ProductOrderItem>
    </CustomerOrder>
</CustomerOrderMessage>
```

Figure 3-12   Instantiation of CharacteristicValue

> **NOTE**   In Figure 3-12, the specification key `specId` points to a single characteristic spec-ification per category of characteristics. This allows alleviating the lack of strong typing in the flexible message structure by providing means of controlling the content on the con-sumer and provider side.

Additional Techniques for Information Model Flexibility

We saw, in the previous section, the means to make business entity attributes variable; however, entities are, in most cases, part of an information graph. What then may happen is that a consumer of one entity is affected indirectly by structural changes of entities referenced indirectly through the graph. The impact is that programs or services that use that entity have to enter a development life cycle and be regenerated and tested, just because the structure of an entity that they reference has been modified.

If the entities are part of different information domains such as customer and products, the ref-erences in the graphs introduce cross domain dependencies. A natural thought is then to introduce keys that give an indirect reference to the other domains. Keys seem obvious to database designers, but many object-oriented models or XML schemas do not formalize a key as a clearly identified attribute because the implicit relationships in the models do not always require this formalization. So keys seem a good way of pointing to another domain without an explicit relationship. However, a simple include file with a typedef in C or C++, a package include in Java with a key object on an inter-face, or a key/keyref definition in XML files can affect the consumers of the key.

So, we have to be careful using keys for sharing model referential integrity that would imply a loss of flexibility and propagation of changes from one information domain or subdo-main to another domain. As shown in Figure 3-13, using explicit key typing induces changes that propagate from one information domain to another domain and may generate high-impact testing and validation costs.

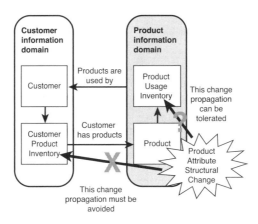

Figure 3-13   Propagation of structural changes between domains

This change propagation blocking also induces the need for exposing only essential information in the information sharing space and provides a means to access details when required. We need then to find a simple but standardized way to point to that data indirectly with a key. This method must recognize that the type definition of the key does affect the clients of that entity, directly or indirectly.

Introducing Loose Coupled Keys in Information Models for Modularity

This is where the notion of URI quoted at the beginning of this chapter is important. As stated in the RFC 3305, "An identifier might specify the location of a resource (a URL) or its name (a URN), independent of location."[9] As a consequence, a reference between information domains or between rather independent subdomains should be a string or text/XML in the form of a URI. Thus, there is no type propagation on the references between domains, and they can evolve without impacting their references.

This way of connecting domains with keys identifying the core entities also requires that the enterprise or the actors' network agree on the semantic content of the unique identifier. For a customer that is a person, it is the social security ID. However, this identifier is country-specific. There are may be multiple choices such as ISO20022,[10] the standard for financial industry messages that define four identifiers for an account (BBAN, IBAN, UPIC, or proprietary). The enterprise should select its primary choice for an identifier and how it creates references to the other possible identifications.

Now let's look at translating that in XML. The first standard that helps us do that is the XML linking language, which as the standards says "allows elements to be inserted into XML documents in order to create and describe links between resources."[11] XLink also defines the relationships and the roles between the structural elements.

XLink is used heavily in the XBRL (eXtensible Business Reporting Language) financial reporting language, and XBRL provides an identifying tag in the exchanges that occur between the various actors for each individual item of data such as Net Profit. The meaning of these tags is defined by XBRL taxonomies, which are the dictionaries that the language uses and are the categorization schemes for these tags. The XLink definitions then connect the roles and locations in the domains, such as in the XSD and XML file excerpts shown in Figures 3-14 and 3-15 linking the calculation to the long-term debt role defined in the role schema.

```
<link:roleType id="debt3" roleURI="http://xbrl.us/us-
gaap/role/disclosure/DebtCalc3">
<link:definition>460200 - Disclosure - Debt (Long-term Debt by Maturity
Alternative) </link:definition>
```

Figure 3-14   Link role definition in the schema

```
<link:roleRef roleURI="http://xbrl.us/us-gaap/role/disclosure/DebtCalc3"
xlink:href="../elts/us-roles-2008-03-31.xsd#debt3"
xlink:type="simple" />
```

Figure 3-15   Link role usage in the XML files pointing to debt3 in the schema

An example usage of these XBRL standards for reporting is IBM's SEC filing.[12] However, XLink is still not sufficient for the information sharing used in loose coupling because in its base form it relies on schema-defined identities and does not point by itself to a particular element identified by a "key" content in the target document. To formulate it with a database equivalent, XLink can refer to a table column but requires additional constructs to point to a specific line of a table based on the cell content.

This is where the XML Pointer Language (XPointer) comes into play to complement the URI. XPointer is the language defined to express fragment identifiers for any URI reference that locates a resource whose Internet media type is one of text/xml, application/xml, text/xml-external-parsed-entity, or application/xml-external-parsed-entity. XPointer uses an extension of XPath to point to specific elements such as those shown in the Figure 3-16.

```
xlink:href="http://mytelco.com/products.xml#xpointer({//product[@name='DSL'])
)"
```

Figure 3-16   Example of XLink and XPointer reference

NOTE   In Figure 3-16, the "name" becomes a key that is used to locate a particular element in the referenced domain, which in this case is the product domain. The only coupling between the domains is then that products have names that are in a textual format.

A similar approach can be applied to subdomains within an information domain provided that there is a need for having more loosely coupled references.

It is natural to map the XPointer principles described previously to non-XML domains such as relational databases, provided that the column used as a key can be accessed with a textual representation. The example in Figure 3-16 would then be used in the product's database schema to access a product table and select the row where the column "name" contains "DSL" within that table.

Managing Keys and Cross-Referencing in Complex Application Environments

As hinted to in the previous section, the same entity may be identified using different identifiers particularly when aspects of that entity are persisted in different systems such as CRM, Order Fulfillment, Supply Chain, and so on. There is an implicit or explicit cross-reference that represents a relationship correlating at least two or more semantically equivalent forms of one entity. This is represented in different physical formats and may originate from different IT systems.

Relationships are important for mapping information between different representations if no rule is applicable to cover a direct mapping. For example, the product relationship of two different back-end systems maps a product of System A to a product of System B. System A, however, has a different indexing system for its products than System B. This means that a relationship is needed because a simple mapping rule might not cover that particular mapping and will require a key lookup to locate the corresponding data in the other system.

There are several means to maintain this cross-referencing. Based on the business and enterprise requirements these approaches can range from single-entity cross-referencing for transactional and process requirements to a global enterprise information consolidation approach with Master Data Management. Solutions exist in both domains within the industry and can be used in conjunction or separately. A Master Data Management approach is, however, a more fundamental approach for the enterprise as it requires collaboration of all the lines of business handling aspects of the selected core entities or master data of the enterprise.

The core of Master Data Management is housed within the various systems and applications that instantiate and utilize the data. Each application has its own discrete function and method for creating, accessing, and analyzing data relating to common enterprise core entities, and these methods are all independent of similar data within other applications.

To address the root cause of this master data complexity multiform Master Data Management centralizes the common data functionality dealing with master data. This strategy allows enterprises to identify common functionality for all systems and applications by supporting all the various ways in which those applications may use master data. More information on solutions for this approach can be found on the IBM Master Data Management site.[13] A lighter approach is a process, capability, or use case approach that consolidates identities and keys based on specific requirements but may then be reusable for further extended use.

As an enablement for a process or services-based integration, IBM provides in WebSphere Process Server a relationship service[14] that is both static and dynamic. Figure 3-17 is a screen view of the relationship editor.

The key's cross-references are dynamically maintained by the system, as it gathers resulting keys from adapters on creation in the various systems provided that the related business objects have clearly been identified to the adapters.

Figure 3-17   Key attribute role definition in the relationship management

Metamodel Approaches for Information Variability

Data is sometimes described in terms of layers of instance data, metadata, and metamodels. The base layer is the data itself, or the instance data. This data conforms to a data model or schema, which is described by the metadata. This metadata itself conforms to a model, which is called the metamodel.

Service Data Objects (SDO)[15] is a specification for a programming model that unifies data programming across data source types, provides robust support for common application patterns, and enables applications, tools, and frameworks to more easily query, view, bind, and update introspective data.

SDO uses metadata to define the structure and content of a data model. This model provides the support for capturing the logical composition of any type of representation of the same entity as shown in Figure 3-18.

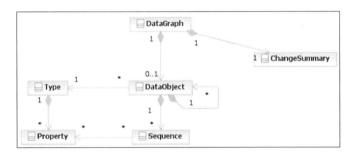

Figure 3-18   UML abstract model of core SDO components

Even if Figure 3-18 is an abstract model used only for accessing physical representations, we can make this abstract model concrete and derive an extremely variable structure to carry messages in the sharing domain. What is proposed here is not the initial proposed use of SDO, and I recommend reading first "Introduction to Service Data Objects" from the standards site.[16]

Figure 3-19 shows the XML schema resulting from using the abstract UML model shown in Figure 3-18 for a materialization of the abstraction principles.

We can use the schema in Figure 3-19 to carry the same Customer Order information payload that was exposed previously in Figure 3-12.

Using this model, as shown in Figure 3-20, the payload becomes metadata driven and of course suffers from expansion. The advantage is that the structure is now independent of the information source, but still reflects both the source semantics and the content that needs to be exchanged.

```
<?xml version="1.0" encoding="UTF-8"?><xsd:schema
targetNamespace="http://SDO/"
xmlns:xsd="http://www.w3.org/2001/XMLSchema" xmlns:sdo="http://SDO/">
  <xsd:complexType name="DataGraph">
    <xsd:sequence>
      <xsd:element minOccurs="0" name="dataObject"
type="sdo:DataObject"/>
      <xsd:element name="changeSummary" type="sdo:ChangeSummary"/>
    </xsd:sequence>
  </xsd:complexType>
  <xsd:complexType name="DataObject">
    <xsd:sequence>
      <xsd:element name="type" type="sdo:Type"/>
      <xsd:element maxOccurs="unbounded" minOccurs="0" name="sequence"
type="sdo:Sequence"/>
      <xsd:element maxOccurs="unbounded" minOccurs="0"
name="dataObject" type="sdo:DataObject"/>
    </xsd:sequence>
  </xsd:complexType>
  <xsd:complexType name="Type">
    <xsd:sequence>
      <xsd:element maxOccurs="unbounded" minOccurs="0" name="property"
type="sdo:Property"/>
      <xsd:element name="name" type="xsd:string"/>
    </xsd:sequence>
  </xsd:complexType>
  <xsd:complexType name="Property">
    <xsd:sequence>
      <xsd:element name="name" type="xsd:string"/>
      <xsd:element name="value" type="xsd:string"/>
    </xsd:sequence>
  </xsd:complexType>
  <xsd:complexType name="Sequence">
    <xsd:sequence>
      <xsd:element maxOccurs="unbounded" minOccurs="0" name="property"
type="sdo:Property"/>
    </xsd:sequence>
  </xsd:complexType>
  <xsd:complexType name="ChangeSummary"/>
  <xsd:element name="sharedEntityGraph"
type="sdo:DataGraph"></xsd:element>
</xsd:schema>
```

Figure 3-19 XML schema for elements based on an SDO model

```
<?xml version="1.0" encoding="UTF-8"?>
<sdo:sharedEntityGraph xmlns:sdo="http://SDO/"
xmlns:xsi="http://www.w3.org/2001/XMLSchema-instance"
xsi:schemaLocation="http://SDO/ SDO.xsd ">
      <dataObject>
          <type>
              <name>CustomerOrderMessage</name>
          </type>
          <dataObject>
              <type>
                  <name>CustomerOrder</name>
                  <property>
                      <name>id</name>
                      <value>MyOrderIdentifier</value>
                  </property>
              </type>
              <dataObject>
                  <type>
                      <name>CharacteristicValue</name>
                      <property>
                          <name>BundleOrder</name>
                          <value>PHONE BUNDLE</value>
                      </property>
                  </type>
              </dataObject>
              <dataObject>
                  <type>
                      <name>ProductOrderItem</name>
                      <property>
                          <name>id</name>
                          <value>PHONE_RENTAL</value>
                      </property>
                  </type>
                  <dataObject>
                      <type>
                          <name>CharacteristicValue</name>
                          <property>
                              <name>Feature</name>
                              <value>CALL_WAITING" </value>
                          </property>
                      </type>
                  </dataObject>
              </dataObject>
          </dataObject>
      </dataObject>
      <changeSummary/>
</sdo:sharedEntityGraph>
```

Figure 3-20 Metadata driven variability message using a principles of SDO abstract model

Adaptive Business Objects

We end this chapter on information variability with a discussion of the Adaptive Business Object initiative that carries interesting aspects even though it did not gain much success in the industry.

The Adaptive Business Object[17] is a business entity with an explicitly managed state that reacts to events by calling services and is at the confluence of data, process, and services. As such, the ABO is a resource that carries not only its state but also a finite state machine with possible transitions. These transitions are enacted by actions using a CRUD model and events on the business object. Events are one-way services, and the actions and events of the ABO model are represented as services.

One of the principles behind ABOs is that processes are in many cases the manifestation of an entity life cycle, with this entity exposing some services and calling services. Some examples of Adaptive Business Objects are Customer Order, Experiment Record, or Trouble Ticket. For example, Experiment Record states are In Design, Pending, In Perform Experiment, In Analysis, In Clone Experiment, In Modify Experiment, In Archive, In Update, and Experiment. An ABO can be extended to be a combination of something similar to the State Chart XML (SCXML) and the object data model within a single resource. For example, in the pharmaceutical industry, experiments require an extensive partnership, and a wide network of experiments must be performed. To gather and perform experiments, the pharmaceutical company sends the experiment objects together carrying their internal states and allowed transition model.

A serialization of the object resource to a partner informs the partner of the services and the next steps that can be carried on the Experiment Record. Thus, an ABO does not require the partner to deploy a particular process, as the process is within the object. However, the partner has to provide the CRUD services that the ABO and the engine need to operate the transitions on the object.

While some implementation has existed in the past for business to business (B2B) interactions, Adaptive Business Objects have only found traction in a few specific industries such as pharmaceuticals.

Summary

In this chapter, we discussed the impact of information changes on the enterprise applications, processes, and services. We looked at defining the semantics of the information and structuring the data into stable and variable sets. We also differentiated the data used for sharing information from the data owned by particular enterprise domains. Toward the end of this chapter, we also examined various techniques for implementing variability.

This use of variability is often pushed to the extreme, and the pragmatic answer for sharing information is that it necessitates a trade-off between stable entity concepts and variability zones based on the anticipated business evolutions and requirements.

CHAPTER 4

Implementing Variable Services

The circumstances of the world are so variable that an irrevocable purpose or opinion is almost synonymous with a foolish one.

William Shakespeare

Patterns of Service Variability Implementations

Implementing services variability is essential to limit the impact of changes in chains of consumers and providers of services. Understanding why we need to focus on variability is just as important, especially since in the initial intention of Web Services as defined by W3C (and included in the following W3C Web Services Activity Statement), nothing seems to limit flexibility.

> Web services provide a standard means of interoperating between different software applications, running on a variety of platforms and/or frameworks. Web services are characterized by their great interoperability and extensibility, as well as their machine-processable descriptions thanks to the use of XML. They can be combined in a loosely coupled way in order to achieve complex operations. Programs providing simple services can interact with each other in order to deliver sophisticated added-value services.[1]

However, two different interpretations of "interoperating" led to some restrictions on the initial loose coupling and extensibility approach.

The first point of view originated from information and document exchange principles with a contractual approach, where the sender and receiver agree on the nature of the interaction, and the receiver tailors it for his needs and has the means to absorb changes. The second point of view originated from the transactional, object-oriented, remote procedure or method, from Common Object Request Broker Architecture (CORBA) supporters with strict definitions of interfaces in which the sender ensures it's right, and any change in the interface propagates to the consumer. The combination of the two approaches led to the implicit use of the **adapter pattern**, in which both adaptation and interface are used, but the pure document approach is restricted and technical loose coupling is added to the procedural approach.

As defined by the Gang of Four (GoF)—Erich Gamma, Richard Helm, Ralph Johnson, and John Vlissides, the authors of the famous Design Patterns book[2]—an adapter "convert[s] the interface of a class into another interface clients expect. It lets consumers and providers work together that couldn't otherwise because of incompatible interfaces. Because the consumer still sees a precise interface the expected loose coupling ends up being mostly a technical loose coupling, but not really a business level loose coupling."

In our approach to variability, we have to look at ways of making these interfaces extensible from a consumer perspective while also looking at supporting changing implementations from a provider perspective. We also have to ensure that provider components can also be consumers of other components and deliver aggregated value from this chain of components.

Matching this evolution with design patterns implies we have to evolve our service modeling to use a combination of a façade pattern and a bridge pattern, defined here:

- **Façade pattern**—Provides a unified interface to a set of interfaces in a subsystem. A façade defines a high-level interface that makes the subsystem easier to use. This façade then exposes a higher granularity interface than the set of subsystem interfaces it integrates.

- **Bridge pattern**—Decouples an abstraction from its implementation so that the two can vary independently. This decoupling can be at design time or at runtime.

Drilling down to the granularity of services implied by the façade pattern has been addressed previously in this book, where we used a functional decomposition to define a manageable granularity. In this chapter, we focus instead on the means to implement these façades, bridges and components.

Variability and Web Services Description Language

Before we attempt to extend our practice for extensibility, let's look at what the standard Web Services have to offer. Some aspects of the standard Web Services Description Language (WSDL) are not commonly known.

WSDL Operation Patterns

Even though request-response is the most used primitive, four interaction patterns are defined by the WSDL standard:[3]

- **One-way**—The endpoint receives a message. The consumer does not expect a response. This is typically a message-oriented approach as supported by message-oriented middleware.

- **Request-response**—The endpoint receives a message and sends a correlated message.

- **Solicit-response**—The endpoint sends a message and receives a correlated message. In principle, this is an inverted request-response where the consumer becomes the provider.

- **Notification**—The endpoint sends a message. This is an inverted one-way message.

The basic profile of the Web Services-Interoperability (WS-I) standard[4] restricts the patterns used to the first two defined (one-way and request-response), and gives precise instructions on the use of one-way operations with HTTP.

Figure 4-1 shows excerpts from the basic profile.

```
4.5.2 Allowed Operations:

Solicit-Response and Notification operations are not well defined by WSDL 1.1;
furthermore, WSDL 1.1 does not define bindings for them.

R2303 A DESCRIPTION MUST NOT use Solicit-Response and Notification type
operations in a wsdl:portType definition.

..........................

4.7.9 One-Way Operations

There are differing interpretations of how HTTP is to be used when performing
one-way operations.

R2714 For one-way operations, an INSTANCE MUST NOT return a HTTP response that
contains an envelope. Specifically, the HTTP response entity-body must be
empty.

R2750 A CONSUMER MUST ignore an envelope carried in a HTTP response message in
a one-way operation.

R2727 For one-way operations, a CONSUMER MUST NOT interpret a successful HTTP
response status code (i.e., 2xx) to mean the message is valid or that the
receiver would process it. ... the Profile specifies that "200" and "202" are the
preferred status codes that the sender should expect, signifying that the one-
way message was received.
```

Figure 4-1   WS-I allowed interpretations for one-way operations

An often omitted extensibility is to use one-way operations to support asynchronous messaging patterns where the only requirement is to specify an input abstract message and defining an output or error handling message is not required. As shown in Figure 4-2, the input element specifies the abstract message format for the one-way operation.

```
<wsdl:definitions .... > <wsdl:portType .... > *
        <wsdl:operation name="nmtoken">
            <wsdl:input name="nmtoken"? message="qname"/>
        </wsdl:operation>
    </wsdl:portType >
</wsdl:definitions>
```

Figure 4-2   One-way messaging in WSDL standard

Another extension is to use the request-response or one-way interactions to exchange bulk information for batch processing. However, in a batch processing case, you should separate the bulk information using attachments to avoid any lengthy intermediary processing of the SOAP messages. The attachment support for interoperability is specified by WS-I in the attachment profile.[5] One of the advantages of having attachments is the ability to include data in a separate MIME part and refer to it from the SOAP envelope as a URI. The attachment profile defines a schema type, `ref:swaRef`, that can be used in a WSDL description to define a message part, and then the URI points to the attachment in the same MIME package.

WSDL Limited Ad-Hoc Polymorphism

To enable these uniform interfaces or operations to vary in their life cycle without affecting the interface consumer, a form of ad-hoc polymorphism is required that allows the same interface to accept varying information types as payloads. We could define our services operation as modern programming languages do with function overloading, where the same function or operation name may carry different information types. The initial WSDL standard did not exclude operation overloading, but the various implementations did not all support it, so interoperability of services became an issue. As a consequence, the WS-I standard explicitly disallowed it in its basic profile shown in Figure 4-3.

```
5.4.3 Distinctive Operations
Operation name overloading in a wsdl:portType is disallowed by the Profile.
R2304 A wsdl:portType in a DESCRIPTION MUST have operations with distinct
values for their name attributes
```

Figure 4-3   WS-I basic profile exclusion of overloading

Similarly, the Service Component Architecture (SCA) standard from the Open SOA consortium also excludes overloading from certain implementation languages[6] as described in Figure 4-4.

```
The style of remotable interfaces is typically coarse grained and intended for
loosely coupled interactions. Remotable service Interfaces are not allowed to
make use of method overloading.
```

Figure 4-4   Exclusion of overloading from SCA C++ remotable interfaces

This restriction is an important limit for variability life cycle as it implies that there cannot be additions of signatures for a given operation after the service has been deployed and is in use. It pushes variability back to the design phase of the WSDL or SCA-based services in the services messages definition, where the information structure has to absorb the variations using techniques described in Chapter 3, "Implementing Dynamic Enterprise Information," and using simple inheritance support in XML schemas. Figure 4-5 shows an international purchase order example that contains U.K. addresses with a specific post code or U.S. addresses with a Zip code and state.

The international purchase order schema shown in Figure 4-6 refers to the address type and moves it into a separate schema to which additional countries may be added in the future.

An interface using a purchase order does not need to know the specific address details; all the interface simply needs to specify is a generic address. Of course, when the purchase order request is generated, specific addresses that have different formats must be produced. The resolution of the real type is done upon serialization by the client. That serialization introduces **xsi:type** in the XML document so that the provider knows what variety of address the element is. This is

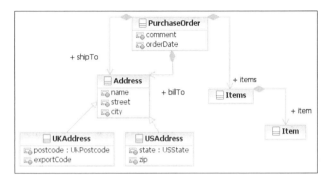

Figure 4-5   Address inheritance example

```
<include    schemaLocation="address.xsd"/> <!-- include address
constructs -->
 <element name="purchaseOrder" type="ipo:PurchaseOrderType"/>
 <complexType name="PurchaseOrderType">
  <sequence>
   <element name="shipTo"    type="ipo:Address"/>
   <element name="billTo"    type="ipo:Address"/>
   <element name="items"     type="ipo:Items"/>
  </sequence>
  <attribute name="orderDate" type="date"/>
 </complexType>
```

Figure 4-6   International purchase order schema

perfectly supported by the WSDL standard and WS-I; however, one should verify that the derived
types are generated with the xsi:type by the serialization. One way to enforce this is to define the
address as abstract with **abstract="true"** in the XML schema; when performing serialization by
the client, the use of abstract in the XML schema is implementation dependent.

Such serialization is shown in Figure 4-7.

```
<ipo:purchaseOrder   orderDate="01-01"
      xmlns:xsi="http://www.w3.org/2001/XMLSchema-instance"
      xmlns:ipo="http://www.example.com/IPO"
      xsi:schemaLocation="http://www.example.com/IPO/ipo.xsd">
  <shipTo exportCode="1" xsi:type="ipo:UKAddress">
         <name>Helen Zoe</name>         <street>47 Eden Street</street>
         <city>Cambridge</city>         <postcode>CB1 1JR</postcode>
  </shipTo>
  <billTo xsi:type="ipo:USAddress">
         <name>Robert Smith</name>        <street>8 Oak Avenue</street>
         <city>Old Town</city>          <state>AR</state>
<zip>95819</zip>
  </billTo>
  <items>
        <item partNum="833-AA">
            <productName>Lapis necklace</productName>
<quantity>1</quantity>
            <USPrice>99.95</USPrice>   <shipDate>1999-12-05</shipDate>
        </item>
  </items>
</ipo:purchaseOrder>
```

Figure 4-7   Sample purchase order with two addresses concrete types

In addition to the ad-hoc input and output message polymorphism, the attachments can
provide versatility. Any additional data content in attachments can be defined as weakly typed

text/XML referenced by a URI. It is then the responsibility of consumer and provider to agree on the attachment structure.

Service Component Architecture

When looking at solutions based on services, service consumers and service providers should not place importance on their respective technologies. Flexibility is enabled by modularity, and therefore instead of having monolithic service consumers accessing monolithic service providers, the modularity leads to smaller, manageable elements. These elements are then what we call components, which can be service providers but also consume services from another provider and so on.

All components should integrate with other components, without knowing how the other components are implemented. Particularly, it should be easy to replace one component with another one, or to provide implementation alternatives based on context and not by interface.

A service component is, in essence, the encapsulation of some business logic that does not preclude a particular language or protocol. The business services it provides can be implemented in variety of technologies such as COBOL transactions, C++, EJBs, Plain Old Java Objects, BPEL processes, and PHP using whatever communication protocol and data format are appropriate. In addition to the business level definition of component interfaces, the exchanged information can be described with an abstraction of the information content represented in any variety of physical formats, such as COBOL copybooks, C structures, Java objects, and so on.

The behavior of the components should be externalized as much as possible in the metadata and can be configured at development time, but preferably at deployment or runtime. These requirements led to the Service Component Architecture (SCA) and Services Data Objects (SDO) standards. This standard is now controlled by the Open SOA collaboration, representing an informal group of major industry leaders.

Service Component Architecture Specifications

Service Component Architecture (SCA) defines:

- An assembly model
- A policy framework including transaction policies and security in the future
- Component implementations for Java and Spring
- Client and implementation for BPEL, COBOL, C, and C++
- Bindings for Web Services, JMS, EJB Session Bean, and JCA (J2EE Connector Architecture)
- Integration specifications for Java EE in addition to the specific J2EE bindings

The assembly model consists of a series of artifacts that define the configuration of an SCA system. It relates specifically to the service components implemented and/or the use of services, and the connections and related artifacts that describe how they are linked together.

Services Components and Composites

SCA components consist of a configured implementation instance for a particular interface definition. The wiring of a component to services provided by another component and the definition of properties required completes the component. Components expose interfaces and consume interfaces. SCA defines a Service Component Description Language (SCDL) as the technology-independent format for describing component implementations and abstracting the users of these descriptions from implementation technology.

SCA composites are assemblies of SCA components with configuration elements. The SCA Composite Model is recursive, and composites can include other composites. The SCA composites define a visibility boundary that is useful to avoid exposing finer grained components in a component assembly. Figure 4-8 is an example of SCA composite as captured in the tooling.

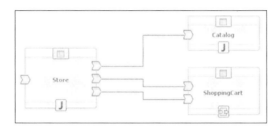

Figure 4-8   Example of an SCA composite with three components

The metadata provided by a component implementation is strictly separated from the metadata provided by the user of a component implementation.

As shown in Figure 4-9, only the services and references are the base for the graphic composite definition shown in Figure 4-8.

```
<?xml version="1.0" encoding="UTF-8"?>
<composite xmlns="http://www.osoa.org/xmlns/sca/1.0"
xmlns:pre="http://store" autowire="false" name="SCAStore"
targetNamespace="http://store">
  <component name="Store">
    . . .
    <service name="StoreService">  . . . </service>
    <reference name="catalog" target="Catalog/CatalogService"/>
    <reference name="shoppingCart" target="ShoppingCart/CartService"/>
    <reference name="shoppingTotal"
target="ShoppingCart/TotalService"/>
  </component>
  <component name="Catalog">
    . . .
    <service name="CatalogService">      . . .      </service>
  </component>
  <component name="ShoppingCart">
    . . .
    <service name="CartService">      . . .      </service>
    <service name="TotalService">      . . .      </service>
  </component>
</composite>
```

Figure 4-9   Services and references in SCDL

SCA achieves separation with separate file formats for describing component implementations and component integration. Exposed services and consumed references define their communication with other applications. The `<service>` and `<reference>` tags in the SCDL do not specify anything about the communication protocols. The communication protocols do not need to be explained as they will derive from the component interface described in the next section.

In the composite SCDL in Figure 4-9, the service exposed by Store is `StoreService`, referencing one target service in the catalog component and two target services in the shopping cart component.

Defining Component Interfaces

The element still missing is how the interfaces access the services. However, SCA does not redefine an interface definition language (IDL).[7] It provides the support to reuse existing IDL interfaces to define the business function signature provided by services and used by the references. There will only be one interface used by other components. To avoid conflicts in the definition of that interface, it will contain one or more operations with optional input and output. In the base standard, SCA only specifies Java interfaces, WSDL 1.1 portTypes, and WSDL 2.0 interfaces but defines an extensibility pattern to enable any other interface types.

Figure 4-10 is an example of a potential interface definition using both WSDL and Java interfaces as specified by the `interface.java` and `interface.wsdl` tags.

```
<component name="Store">
    . . .
    <service name="StoreService">
       <interface.wsdl
interface="http://book/#wsdl.interface(StoreType)"/>
    . . .
    </service>
</component>
<component name="Catalog">
    . . .
    <service name="CatalogService">
       <interface.java interface="catalog.sca.jdbc.CatalogService"/>
    . . .
    </service>
</component>
<component name="ShoppingCart">
    . . .
    <service name="CartService">
       <interface.wsdl
interface="http://book/#wsdl.interface(CartType)"/>
    . . .
    </service>
    <service name="TotalService">
       <interface.wsdl
interface="http://book/#wsdl.interface(TotalType)"/>
    . . .
    </service>
</component>
```

Figure 4-10   Interfaces in SCA components

It is worthwhile to note that some SCA implementations, such as PHP, enable a dynamic interface definition in which the WSDL corresponding to a PHP service is communicated as the result of an HTTP request.[8]

Integrating Component with Bindings

Now we need the composite to specify the communication between the components with which it integrates. This is the purpose of bindings.

SCA binding defines which communication protocols should be used between the components in a composite. When bindings are not specified, default binding are used that are specific to the SCA runtime engines. As already mentioned, the SCA standard defines bindings for other Web Services, JMS, EJB Session Bean, and JCA. Each remotable service and each reference may specify the protocols it supports using bindings as shown in Figure 4-11.

```
<component name="Store">
    . . .
    <service name="StoreService">
        . . .
        <binding.ws
wsdlElement="http://book/#wsdl.port(StoreService/Store)"/>
        <binding.ejb ejb-version="EJB3"/>
    </service>
    . . .
</component>
<component name="Catalog">
    . . .
    <service name="CatalogService">
        . . .
        <binding.ejb ejb-version="EJB3"/>
    </service>
</component>
<component name="ShoppingCart">
    . . .
    <service name="CartService">
        <binding.ws wsdlElement="http://
book/#wsdl.port(CartService/Cart)"/>
    </service>
    <service name="TotalService">
        . . .
        <binding.ws wsdlElement="http://
book/#wsdl.port(TotalService/Total)"/>
    </service>
</component>
```

Figure 4-11   WSDL and EJB bindings in a composite definition

Figure 4-11 shows an extract where the bindings in the composite definition of represented in Figure 4-8 are binding.ws and binding.ejb. The extensibility point here is that several bindings can be configured for the same component, allowing the selection of the best binding to the target component based on nonfunctional requirements.

Interestingly, SCA for PHP defines an extensive list of bindings: binding.ebaysoap, binding.jsonrpc, binding.message (alternative to JMS), binding.restresource, binding.restrpc, binding.simpledb, binding.soap, and binding.xmlrpc.[9]

Now that we've specified how our components communicate, we have to define how they connect to the logic that implements the services.

Making Component Concrete with Implementation

SCA implementation defines the concrete implementation technology and instantiation properties for a given component exposing services. There is a wide selection of implementation types, such as Java, Spring, COBOL, PHP, BPEL, or C++. Another composite could also be the implementation that allows fractal models for components.

As shown in Figure 4-12, the store composite includes two components implemented in Java and one implemented as another composite.

```
<component name="Store">
  <implementation.java class="test.StoreImpl"/>
  <service name="StoreService">
    . . .
  </service>
</component>
<component name="Catalog">
  <implementation.java requires="managedTransaction.local"
class="catalog.sca.jdbc.CatalogServiceImpl"/>
  <service name="CatalogService">
    . . .
  </service>
</component>
<component name="ShoppingCart">
  <implementation.composite requires="" name="pre:SCACart"/>
  <service name="CartService">
    . . .
  </service>
  <service name="TotalService">
    . . .
  </service>
</component>
</composite>
```

Figure 4-12   Java and composite implementations

We now have a completed definition of the composition of the components as well as its interfaces and bindings. But the conditions and context of use of the component may vary and require specific protocols, transactional, or security aspects. This is achieved with the SCA policy framework.

Controlling Component and Composite Behavior with Policies

The behavior of components can be specified by externalized policy means. The SCA standard addresses this domain with policies, intents, and policy sets.

SCA policies define a particular capability or constraint capability, or even a constraint that can be applied to service such as encryption between two components.

SCA intents are used to describe the abstract policy requirements regarding the Quality of Service (QoS) specific to a component. These can address the component behavior itself or any external references the component interacts with. The application deployer will specify what policy set covers that intent for a specific deployment purpose. You can see in Figure 4-13 a "requires" attribute in the implementation, which is a reference to a policy intent specifying the type of transactional support required.

The SCA security standard defines three intents:

1. **Authentication** specifies whether the client must authenticate to use an SCA service.

2. **Confidentiality** is used to control the hiding or encryption of the contents of a message from anyone other than the consumer and provider.

3. Integrity is the last security intent that defines the need for providing tampering protection for the message, such as that provided by an XML-signature support.

As more than one policy can apply to one given component in a given context, the SCA policy sets then group the SCA policies that target concrete use in specific SCA bindings and implementations.

SCA tools provide interfaces to manage policies and intents. The example in Figure 4-13 is constructed from the preferences panel provided with the Rational Application Developer SCA Development Tools, which allows specification of default intents for constructing SCA components and composites.

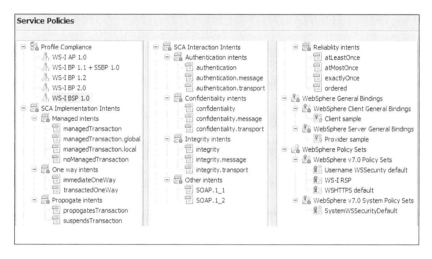

Figure 4-13   Sample list of intents in SCA tooling

Using this tooling, the service component developer can graphically select the intents and policies that are required for a particular component.

Annotating Code for Service Exposure

Each implementation has its own specific annotation to help expose services. Here, we list just a few useful examples.

There are cases where the service component implementer will defer the wiring to a dynamic binding layer, as an example with dynamic binding performed in an enterprise services bus. This is supported by the use of the annotation @wiredByImpl that defines the use of a stub for the component and not the final wiring resolved at runtime.

Even though the service can sometimes be inferred from the service class in Java, a programmer may explicitly specify the services provided using the @Service annotation. Similarly, PHP uses also an @service annotation, but it appears differently in the code in a comment preceding the class definition. COBOL also defines annotations in comments such as the @Service annotation shown in Figure 4-14.

```
Java: The annotation is in the body
@Service ( CatalogService.class ) public class CatalogService
implements ICatalogService { }

PHP: The annotation appears in a comment
/**
 * @service
 * @binding.ws
 */
class CatalogService { }

COBOL: The annotation appears in a comment
 IDENTIFICATION DIVISION.
 PROGRAM-ID. CATS0001.
 * @Service name="CatalogService"
 * interface="ICatalogService"
```

Figure 4-14   Code annotation for services identification in different languages

For details on all the possible annotations, refer to the specific language implementation standards on the Open SOA site (http://www.osoa.org/display/Main/Home).

REST Services

In our quest for services variability, we can look to the World Wide Web model's ability to scale to see its enormous success is, in fact, due to its variability. The Uniform Resource Identifiers (URIs) and HTTP standards simplicity are at the base of this success. REpresentational State Transfer (REST) is the architectural model of the World Wide Web. "The key abstraction of information in REST is a resource," states Roy T. Fielding, one of Apache's cofounders, in his dissertation, "Any information that can be named can be a resource."[10]

Defining Services Using REST

When accessing a Web site, only a few method options are available with the specific differentiation coming from the targeted resource.

The HTTP standard defines eight methods that can be applied on the resources located and identified by URIs. These methods are as follows:[11]

- **OPTIONS**—A request for information about the communication options.

- **GET**—Retrieves the information that is identified by a given URI. It is equivalent to the Request in a database CRUD model.

- **HEAD**—Also retrieves information like GET but only metadata in headers and not the body of the information.

- **POST**—Used to send an information entity to the target resource for that resource to handle as an addition. It is equivalent to the Create in a database CRUD model.

- **PUT**—Also used to send information but primarily expects that information to preexist. The target server may create the resource information element if it does exist. It is equivalent to the Update in a database CRUD model.

- **DELETE**—Used to request the deletion of the resource identified by the URI. It is equivalent to the Delete in a database CRUD model.

- **TRACE**—A technical method that allows doing an end-to-end verification of the communication chain between the requester and the provider.

- **CONNECT**—Allows the connection through an Secure Socket Layer (SSL) tunnel.

With the four methods that look at the target resource content, GET, POST, PUT, and DELETE, we then have a generic model with four base services on resources.

The publicized opposition between Web Services and REST is only apparent, since the REST architectural model is about services on resources (or identified elements contained by these resources). Most, if not all, of Web Services are about actions on resources. Given that resources by Fielding's definition are anything that can be named, any scheme that precisely names state transitions of resources can be used as a service equivalent on the containing resource. Semantically, a Web Service is just a parametric state transition request on a target resource.

Examples of Resource Structure

There are multiple ways to define resource structures and to map them to services.

One example is Project Zero, an incubator project to explore the development and delivery of a runtime environment that simplifies the creation of dynamic web applications. This project defines services to manage Web communities' sites.

Project Zero uses a simple REST service model that could look like this example:

```
/resources/<collection name>[/<member identifier>[/<path info>]]
```

Using that model to get information might look like this:

```
GET /resources/people/<peopleId>/accounts/<accountsId>
```

Generalizing that model in a recursive way, any resource element can be accessed and services applied as shown here:

```
/<coll. name>[/<coll. identifier>[/<subcoll. name>[/<subcoll.
identifier>[etc...]]]
```

The structure of the resources can also use the principles of the Management Information Base (MIB) used by most of the system management systems with the Simple Network Management Protocol (SNMP). SNMP uses a protocol that preexisted the Web, but provides a simple and efficient way to access any resource located anywhere. All Management Information Bases are part of an information hierarchy that the Internet Assigned Numbers Authority (IANA) defines (see IANA maintained MIBs on the www.iana.org/protocols site). The hierarchy in an MIB is a resource hierarchy that defines how to name tables and columns and how to derive the numerical object identifiers (OIDs), as shown in Figure 4-15, which represents the hierarchy as a tree with the combination of name and numerical object identifiers.

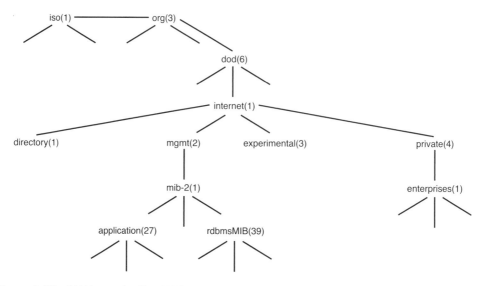

Figure 4-15   IANA standardized MIB structure

For example, the following value is the path to the Application MIB: *iso.org.dod.internet.mgmt.mib-2.application.*

An OID is the numerical equivalent of a path. It uniquely describes each piece of data that an SNMP Network Manager can obtain and is written as a string of numbers separated by periods (.). For example, the following value is the OID for the Application MIB: 1.3.6.1.2.1.27.

It is interesting to see that the SNMP protocol only requires a few verbs to manage all types of infrastructures. These verbs are get, get-next, get-bulk, set, get-response, trap, notification, inform, and report, and they could easily be mapped to a REST HTTP approach.

Handling REST Payload Information with JSON

In the majority of cases, the data used by REST services is the JavaScript Object Notation (JSON). This notation is a lightweight data-interchange format. It is easy for humans to read and write as well for machines to parse and generate. JSON is a name/value pair text format that is completely language independent but uses conventions that are familiar to programmers of the C-family of languages, including C, C++, C#, Java, JavaScript, Perl, Python, and many others.

Figures 4-16 and 4-17 are two examples of JSON input and output used by the WebSphere Business Monitor services. The first JSON message is the one used by the alerts/dashboard update service provided by IBM WebSphere Monitor to update dashboard alerts.

The update dashboard alerts service uses the URI /alerts/dashboardalerts with the POST method, but in that case, the POST request type is used with the X-METHOD-OVERRIDE parameter set to PUT so that it indicates to the REST service that the PUT method should be used instead.

```
[ -- Alert bindings array
  ( -- 1st binding
     "Binding ID": "ABC123",
     "Dashboard": false,
     "Cell": false,
     "E-mail": true,
     "Pager": false
  )
  ( -- next alert binding to be updated
     ...
  )
]
```

Figure 4-16   Sample JSON input message

The exact same URI with a GET instead of a POST/PUT returns the list of subscriptions as shown in Figure 4-17.

```
{
  "Alert Subscription Array": [ -- Alert subscription array
                               ( -- 1st alert binding
                                  "Binding ID": "ABC123",
                                  "Name": "Test Situation Binding",
                                  "Description": "Binding for testing",
                                  "Category": "Test",
                                  "Creation Timestamp": "2007-02-02T15:15:10",
                                  "Creation Timestamp Localised": "2007-02-
02T13:15:10",
                                  "Dashboard": true,
                                  "Cell": false,
                                  "E-mail": false,
                                  "Pager": false
                               )
                               ( -- next alert binding
                                  ...
                               )
                             ],
  "Record Count": 2,
  "Page Size": 10,
  "Page Number": 1
}
```

Figure 4-17   Example JSON response message

Summary

From classical Web Services to more modern Services Component Architecture or REST services, this chapter demonstrated that technology allows the dynamic interpretation of services and the externalization of the behavioral aspects of policies. Technology, therefore, allows the transitioning of business requirement implications to configuration aspects.

These services are sometimes the triggers for processes or in other cases the resulting actions from processes. In either case, these processes require flexibility, which we discuss in the next chapter.

Implementing Dynamic Business Processes

Almost all quality improvement comes via simplification of design, manufacturing...
layout, processes, and procedures.

Tom Peter

Making End-to-End Processes Agile with Modularity

Enterprises must respond quickly and efficiently to shifting market requirements, regulations, and customer needs. In a competitive market, they must look at new products; telecommunication operators who currently provide a triple play—broadband, Internet Voice over IP phones, and IP television—are now looking at providing a quadruple play by adding gaming. They are also looking at providing opportunistic products, such as a Valentine's Day online Web promotion of two mobile phones with unlimited calls between the two mobiles. Therefore, the corresponding order to cash process must be changed to provision gaming on a centralized platform, or the delivery process must be adapted to ship two phones in the same bundle.

At the end of the day, we want to have a palette of atomic or composite services that we can easily and dynamically assemble in business processes to realize new product delivery, deliver to new countries with different legislations, or address new channels. However, even though today's tools make it easy to design and capture a new flow for a business process, there is a software delivery life cycle impact that comes from the transformation of design models to executable models.

Commonly, processes modeled with a process modeling standard (such as XPDL or WS-BPEL) do not end up being interpreted from the design model but rather include a step to transform the process modeling artifacts and documents into an executable model. As a consequence, business processes implemented in workflow or choreography engines have the same testing requirements as the code artifacts for these executable process models. In addition, even though the business process design models use standardized formats that enable interchange, the executable formats are not compatible between vendors.

If we desire business processes to be agile, we must contain the impact of change in smaller modules that are faster and easier to model, deliver as executables, and have a shorter test cycle. In addition, the links between these modules must be dynamic and allow for the easy addition of new lanes of processing without affecting the existing lanes. The end-to-end process becomes then like a train, where each wagon contains a manageable and replaceable process module, pulling the next wagon with a standardized service interaction, only requiring the knowledge of the previous and next links. In Chapter 1, "From Simplified Integration to Dynamic Processes," we saw the enterprise business decomposition; the logical decomposition of processes from APQC in categories, groups, processes, and tasks; and finally, the BPMN categorization of abstract, private, and collaboration processes. Let's now examine a practical use of these approaches to modularize and deliver agile business processes.

Modeling Processes for Dynamicity

As a concrete example to describe the dynamicity approach, I base the following discussion in this chapter on a particular scenario and evolution of the products to show the variability of the process.

In the first scenario, a Customer Sales Representative (CSR) wants to place an order for a triple play: broadband access, Voice over IP telephone, and IP television. Telecommunication operators typically offer this type of bundling.

The system identifies and qualifies the customer according to information provided by the CSR and prompts him with the available product categories and lists (Qualify Customer). The CSR then performs the order entry by selecting the triple play product from the list. Then the CSR performs additional information entry necessary for the triple play such as location of the customer (Update Service Delivery Location). The system performs validation of IP Television for that customer as this service requires a customer to be less than a mile from the physical phone copper line to the Digital Subscriber Line Access Multiplexer physical box (Verify Feasibility). The CSR then selects additional product characteristics such as voice mail or call barring and submits the preorder.

The system also performs credit verification and provides an order summary. The CSR confirms the order on another screen. The system then initiates the order fulfillment through a business process that manages the distribution of the order information to the various downstream applications for service activation (Configure and Activate Service) and resource provisioning (Provision and Deliver Resource) and order progress tracking (Track and Trace Order Handling). At the completion of the provisioning process, the system sends an e-mail to the customer stating that the triple play product is available to her.

In the evolution of the scenario, the telecommunication operator wants to introduce a quadruple play option with gaming and multiplayer gaming options using the set top box complement to the router. This implies a change in the ordering process to provision this new service (Configure and Activate Service) and also to deliver a gamepad or joystick that interacts with the set top box. If the customer already has a set top box that does not support gamepad or joystick (query Customer Inventory), then the process needs to trigger the delivery of a replacement set top box.

As described in the first two chapters, a tree decomposition of the enterprise allows us to identify the common aspects of the process and the variations.

Allocating Use Cases from the Scenario into the Process Tree Decomposition

As mentioned earlier, let's start by transforming the scenario into use cases using the eTOM decomposition.

As you can see in this UML representation, the derivation tree has been represented on the left by a package structure. Here are some example level elements: level 0: Operations; level 1: Customer Relationship Management; level 2: Order Handling; and level 3: Track & Manage Customer Order Handling. Figure 5-1 shows only the tree branches relevant to the preceding scenario selected. Use cases have been identified and allocated to the appropriate tree branches for our scenario.

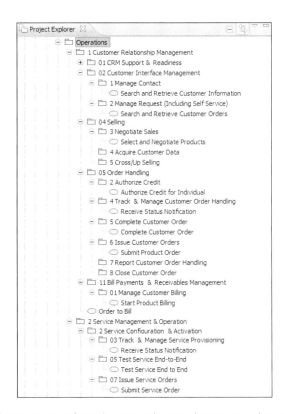

Figure 5-1   Allocating use cases from the scenario onto the process decomposition

As discussed in Chapter 1, the lower level (level 3) use cases are potentially private processes as they have one business owner that defines the rules within that use case. The order to bill use case at level 2 will reference the level 3 use cases and will most likely be a BPMN abstract process with multiple business owners. This process will be realized implicitly by the chaining of lower level use cases but not by running an explicit choreography.

Let's apply these two rules to identify potential services and process articulation points:

1. No private business process should span multiple functional derivation tree branches.

If an abstract process has to do so, it must use a business service operation to reach that branch. That is, no process will explicitly first call Selling/Negotiate Sales/Select and Negotiate Products and then call Order Handling/Issue Customer Orders/Submit Product Order. However, a business service operation must represent the interface to Submit Product Order, and this business service operation is called from Select and Negotiate Products and, by the way, should be bonded dynamically to allow Submit Product Order implementation variations. The difference is subtle and will be explained further.

In the first case, Figure 5-2 shows a Selling process that implements a workflow between the two processes and as a result has an engine waiting for the end of the negotiation chain to trigger the next process. This makes the Selling process dependent on all Order Handling changes or variations of the Submit Customer Order process.

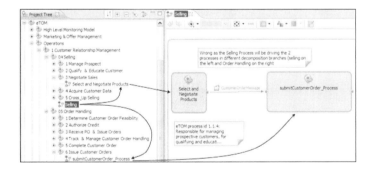

Figure 5-2   BPMN view of selling process crossing decomposition branches

In the dynamic implementation case, there is no more an explicit Selling process but the Select and Negotiate Products process starts with a human task that calls the Submit Customer Order service. But the implementation of the process, could differ based on context or content with variations of the implementation of the process, such as one first variation being Submit Customer Order for Corporate, a second Submit Order for Individual Customers, and maybe a third variation Submit Customer Order for Government (as in the U.S. government must always have a better commercial handling than any other customer).

Then after applying the appropriate dynamic resolution, the Select and Negotiate Products will dynamically be chained to the appropriate implementation. If a process needs to call to a process in another branch at the same level, it does this by calling a business service operation that is a dynamic binding façade to that subsequent process. This removes the correlation between the process implementation and the consumer of the process. Figure 5-3 is a view of this type of chaining between branches.

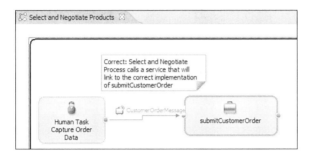

Figure 5-3   BPMN view of chaining between branches using a service interface

In this decomposition diagram, Figure 5-3, we need to add an interface exposing the use case for realization as a private business process. Figure 5-4 shows the interface added to the use case in a UML model.

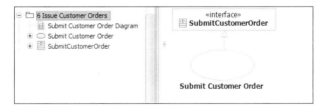

Figure 5-4   UML interface to a use case realization

This private process may itself chain to another process and become a cascading chain of façades. It is not a "chain of responsibility" pattern even though it contains "chain." The basic "chain of responsibility" pattern avoids coupling the sender of a request to its receiver by giving more than one handler a chance to handle the request. However, in our case, we avoid coupling by having process handlers exposed by a façade interface calling the next façade to realize the concrete chain.

Each façade private process implementation handler optionally calls façades to the next private process implementation handler and so on, creating a chain of nested calls that realize the end-to-end abstract process. This pattern could be called a "cascading chain of façades," as shown in Figure 5-5. Façades in the first rule case occur between tree branches that are under the control of different business owners. The façades are the representation of the contracts between these business owners, who each are responsible for the rules and realization in the space they control represented by a branch in the tree decomposition.

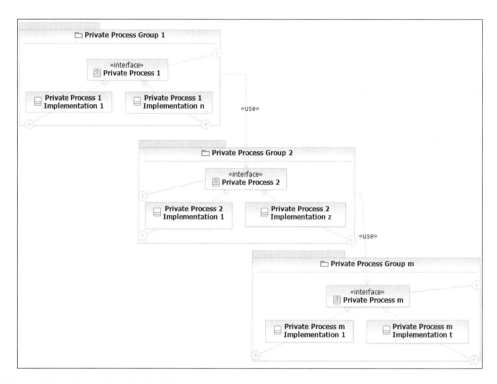

Figure 5-5   Cascading chain of façades

This first rule helps us with variability between different business domains. Now, let's look at how we avoid making processes too dependent on lower level constructs.

2. A business process at a given level (n) should only choreograph subprocesses or services at the immediate level down (n+1).

First, let's note an exception to the rule: When only one service from the lower level sub-branch is consumed and will be the only consumed service in any foreseeable process, it may be called directly. Otherwise, if multiple services or subprocesses are chained at a given level, they must be grouped into a process module in the above level.

This approach is consistent with the Fractal Component Model,[1] which aims at providing a strong separation of concerns to allow modularity and extensibility. The content of a fractal component can be made of other Fractal components nested at an arbitrary level, each exposed with a service interface in the approach that we are taking here. Like the Fractal Component Model, the Fractal Process Model uses the same three specific cases of the separation of concerns principle, namely, separation of interface and implementation (Service Orientation to expose processes), component-oriented programming (process components and modules), and inversion of control (externalization of behavioral control configuration).

There are two patterns of lower layer access. The first pattern is a refinement of a particular activity, task, or service to a specific target realization; the second one is an aggregation of lower level activities into a higher aggregate.

To explain the first pattern, let's take the example of resource reservation where these resources can be telephone numbers or e-mail addresses. eTOM process decomposition tells us that resource reservation occurs in the Allocate & Install Resource level 3 process. However, within that level 3, we need a resource reservation that is independent of resource type, the specific type being handled at a lower level of granularity. In most current implementations, the specific lower level interfaces are bound dynamically to the upper interface using content based routing that looks for the resource type to determine what lower level interface should be used to realize the level 3 reserve resource interface (see Figure 5-6).

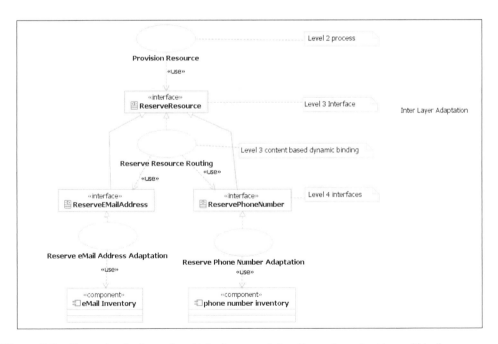

Figure 5-6   Example of a lower level interface resolution through content based binding

The second pattern is a when a higher level process reflects sequences of actions that are much deeper in the tree. To explain that pattern, take the example of customer calling for a service request, which could be connection of a house to the power supplier or a change in the power supply plan. The corresponding APQC category is Deliver Product and Services, and Figure 5-7 shows the decomposition to the task level defined in the APQC Process Classification Framework.

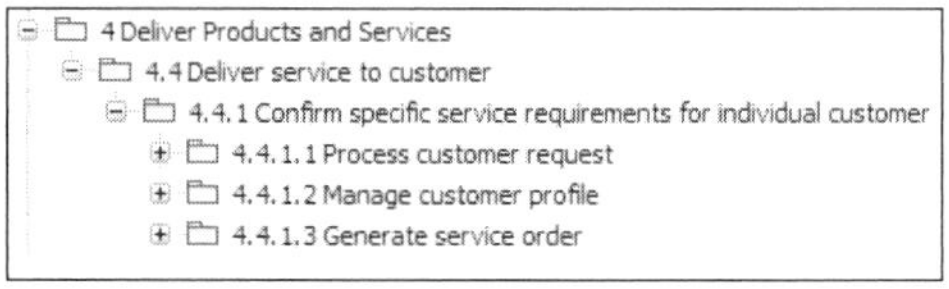

Figure 5-7   Example of tree decomposition

The process first must look at the type of request, then manage the profile, and finally submit the appropriate service order, if it is a service order.

Figure 5-8 shows that the sequence to verify whether a customer exists happens in the profile management process and occurs within the 4.4.1.2 task but is exposed to the 4.4.1 process level. This makes the process dependent on that task implementation and as an example any profile management change would propagate to any process using profile management.

In a reusable and modular approach, we recommend encapsulating the profile management activity sequences in a module exposed as a service to the tree level above. This leads to a much simpler process flow that is now consistent with the process decomposition approach and provides much more agility in replacing specific lower level behavior by alternative options depending on context (such as self service profile management from the Web, or differentiating profile management in call center and in a branch).

Figure 5-9, representing that flow, handles the Manage Customer Profile elements separately, with a potential variable implementation as described in the first pattern (refinement of a particular activity) discussed previously.

Realizing Private Processes as Application Components

At the bottom level and cross levels, services shown in business processes are consumed from an idealized application map layer and identified from the process decomposition but packaged per implementation domain. To give a concrete example, an order handling process needs to look at customer information and product catalog, service order management, and billing account management applications, which define the overarching structure for services.

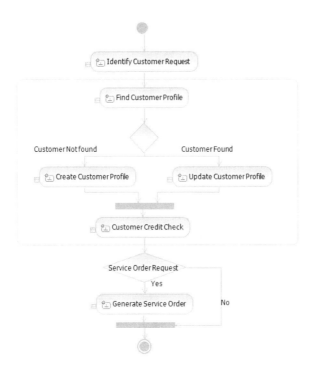

Figure 5-8   Example of process model dependent on lower level activities

Figure 5-9   Decomposition level consistent process

As represented in Figure 5-10, the Track & Manage Customer Order Handling eTOM level 3 process calls submitServiceOrder in the Service Order Management application and also calls the established SLA in the Service Level Agreement application.

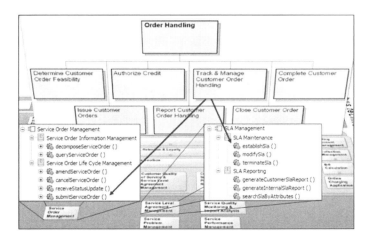

Figure 5-10   Packaging of services per application domain

If we grouped these services into a package aligned with Track & Manage Customer Order Handling, we would only reflect the consumer view and not the essence of the functions carried by the services. By packaging the service operations into services that are aligned with an application implementation we have a more natural life cycle management of those services.

As mentioned in Chapter 1, it is essential to have an idealized application map. This map of applications materializes the intersection of high-level process categories and information domains, such as fulfillment processes and customer information, into an implementation domain. The map also helps define a target for application restructuring, using the services as a transition mode and isolation layer.

Table 5-1 is an example of the organization of services into applications after the exposed operations have been identified from a process functional decomposition, use case, and sequence flow analysis.

Table 5-1   Organization of Services

Application Domain	Application Component	Business Service	Exposed Operation
Service Configuration Management	Service Order Management	Manage Service Order Lifecycle	submitServiceOrder
			receiveStatusUpdate

Table 5-1 Organization of Services

Application Domain	Application Component	Business Service	Exposed Operation
			amendServiceOrder
			cancelServiceOrder
		Manage Service Order Information	queryServiceOrder
			decomposeServiceOrder
	Service Activation Management	Manage Customer Facing Services	configureCustomerFacingService
			activateCustomerFacingService
			deactivateCustomerFacingService
		Manage Resource Facing Services	configureResourceFacingService
			activateCustomerFacingService
			deactivateResourceFacingService

The benefit of having such application domain and component alignment is also to enable the definition of vocabularies and behavioral rules per functional domain.

The reason for having such packaging with an idealized application layer is to provide an isolation layer that enables the consuming processes to be made independent of real application implementations. Thus the idealized application exposes a layer of generic and variable services that hide the implementation from the consumer and do whatever adaptation is necessary behind that service façade. In Chapter 6, "Implementing the Enterprise Expansion Joint," we address the techniques and the practices for implementing such a flexible integration layer.

Additional Techniques for Process Variability

In the previous sections, we looked at the overall modularization and granularity approach to achieve process variability. However, we can achieve further dynamicity and variability by working on the process implementation itself and the technical constituents of a process. All these techniques look at reducing the impact of change whether it is a change to behavior, payload, or context.

Business Rule Engines

A first category of variability improvement is provided by an externalization of the behavior from code or models into configuration, policies, or property files that can be changed at runtime. These configurations, policies, and/or files require less testing because their management cycle comes later in the Software Development Life Cycle. These business rules express business policies as a list of conditions to meet before performing a list of actions.

The supporting middleware is usually qualified as a business rules engine. When looking at using rules externalization in business processes, we must be careful to not add additional dependency that increases the life cycle. Thus, the interactions with rules engines must be defined as services, whether it is the process that calls the rules execution through services, or the rules engine execution calling services as resulting actions.

These rules engines use models and functional domains for which there are standards initiatives somehow converging on several domains. The rules semantics are defined by the Semantics of Business Vocabulary and Business Rules (SBVR) standard from OMG looking at ontologies and vocabularies. The exchange format is the focus of the W3C Rule Interchange Format (RIF) or Web Ontology Language (OWL), and the runtime aspects and APIs are addressed by JSR 94 Java API. SBVR is a metamodel specification for capturing expressions in a controlled natural language and representing them in formal logic structures.

Even though these standards provide some convergence, rules engines differences still apply, and there will be a gradation of usage and capabilities. There is no standardized rules classification, but here is a summary of the typical set:

1. Simple rule: If condition is met, then perform some action.

2. Rule set: Perform action if all conditions of a set of rules are met with no sequence implied between the rules.

3. Rule sequence: Evaluates all rules in a linear sequence and perform action if all rules conditions are met (used for compliance, validation).

4. Decision tables: In a decision table, more than one condition decides the action. The conditional logic is represented in a table where the rows and columns intersect to determine the appropriate action. Each column represents a condition. In a decision table, several conditions may get evaluated, but only one action is acted on.

5. Rule rete[2]: Plexus of rules where each rule has a dependency on at least one case of multiple predecessors; otherwise, it would be a sequence (used for correlation). The action is driven by the concentration of the rules' affluent to one last rule.

6. Other inference rules: Rules that have no organized dependencies and which the system needs to combine to determine whether the resulting condition is met.

7. Rules flow: An equivalent of a process or a workflow with branches and decision points where the next rule depends on the previous rule evaluation result.

8. Complex event processing: Where the rules add time dependencies and events to the rules. For example, if a credit card is used in a New York retail shop and then in a Texas shop in less than one hour, the credit card is a false credit card.

The same modularization that applies to private processes boundaries must be applied to sets, sequences, or flows of rules to avoid mixing business ownership of rules in different domains. Then the action of the rules can be effective or informative, meaning that the rule action consists of providing information on the evaluation of the conditions, or can call a method or service to have a direct effect on the result of the evaluation.

In the first case, the rules engine is usually called as a service just to evaluate a business condition on information passed to the engine as a service interaction and return the evaluation, and then in the calling process take some decision based on the result of the rules evaluation. In the second case, the rules themselves can drive more complex actions and can be information model changes or external service or method calls that are fired when the rules detect that the appropriate conditions are met.

The following examples (see Figure 5-11 through Figure 5-13) give you a more thorough idea of some of the rule sets discussed previously. A simple rule example is a comparison with a value that returns true or false such as a loan approval limit amount check, as shown in Figure 5-11.

Figure 5-11   Simple rule returning Boolean

Because the limit amount may change, it has to be configurable at runtime, and a template is defined to replace the above 50000 value with whatever the LoanValue variable will be set to in the configuration user interface after the rules component has been deployed.

The example in Figure 5-12 using SBVR shows a rule that detects if the customer selects IPTV, it requires DSL broadband. It also detects which action modifies the information model accordingly. The vocabulary has previously defined elements from the information model, such as "product order" or "product order line item" and attributes such as "name."

Figure 5-13 is a rule flow, consisting of a workflow of tasks that check the credit of a customer and select an appropriate insurance package based on the credit check rules verification result. Such rules flows should be kept in rules engines only if they consist of a cascade of rule checks packaged as a global rule. Otherwise, it is preferable to use more services-oriented chore-ography engines and standards, such as WS-BPEL.

> If the product order contains a product order line item wih name "IPTV" and there is no product order line item with name "DSL" Then add product order line item "DSL" to the product order

Figure 5-12   Rule acting on product selection to define product dependency

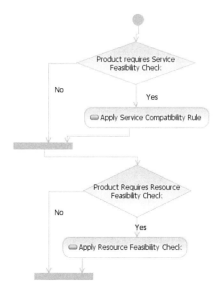

Figure 5-13   Example of rule flow in a UML activity diagram

This type of diagram is available from specific diagram builders in products such as Ilog JRules. In this type of flows rules can be conditionally applied based on the path that the rules evaluation resolves at each step. This can be used to build complex combinations of rules.

Extracting Routing Logic from Business Processes

In Figure 5-6 earlier in the chapter, we described a pattern that exposes to a process a higher level interface with the implementation of a more dynamic selection of the target service implementation.

Pursuing further simplification of the business processes to limit the cost of maintenance, the selection of target service endpoints can be removed from these processes to allow an externalized policy based selection. This alternative to maintaining binding choices is to use parametric bindings based on characteristics. Instead of a service consumer interacting directly with a service, the service is called through an endpoint assembly layer that may make an endpoint selection routing decision based on content of the service payload, context of the call such as incoming channel information, or contract such as response time or availability of the target end-point.

For example, in a triple play provisioning each of the specific processes for DSL, IPTV, or Voice over IP is exposed using the same interface. Adding the routing logic in the calling process makes this process dependent on the target endpoint and would require a process to change the day a "gaming" fourth play needs to be added to the possible bundles.

Since the variable payload contains the required service name it is much simpler for the calling process to loop on the set of included service orders and call the same service interface for each included service order deferring the appropriate service endpoint selection to a policy based routing layer configurable at runtime. In this case the routing will be performed based on the Service Name.

This endpoint routing layer is a semantic aware extension of an enterprise service bus, usually using ontologies to characterize the policies. The calling process logic is simplified, and additional service endpoints can be added with the appropriate policies to dynamically make decisions on the endpoints you want to invoke, based on the interface that is requested and the costs for those endpoints.

As you can see in Figure 5-14, after the endpoint selection and routing has been made there may still be the need to adapt the granularity of the exposed interface to the bottom-up reality of the applications. This adaptation needs to be performed as close as possible to the application to potentially handle units of work or manage state of data that is not exposed by the to interfaces but still needs to be preserved in the interactions. As already mentioned this topic requires specific consideration, and we address policy based endpoint matchmaking, granularity, and variability adaptation and matchmaking techniques in Chapter 6.

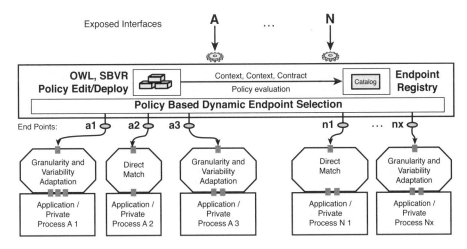

Figure 5-14   Policy based dynamic endpoint selection

Limiting Information Model Impact on Business Processes

We discussed in Chapter 3, "Implementing Dynamic Enterprise Information," the introduction of variability in the information model, but this might still not be enough to reduce the impact of information changes on the processes.

In too many cases, I have been confronted with the change impact on processes because of indirect changes in the information structure. Even though tools make changes easy in process models, the deployment life cycle often involves a costly system test phase triggered by changes that have no direct relationship with the processes.

In consequence, processes should only carry the decisional information subset, so that changes of information that attribute structure not related to decision flows do not affect the processes. This is also where information as a service starts playing a more important role to separate the pure information persistence roles from the process flows.

For example, instead of carrying the full customer information through customer order processing, a customer key identifier and just location information can be sufficient to handle the order process. If any integrated application needs more information in its specific interfaces, it can use mediation in the bus or adaptation layer to retrieve that information using the key identifier and then call the target interface. This pushes the information dependency closer to the target integration points instead of adding a dependency on the private processes.

Figure 5-15 shows an example of separation of decisional data from the other information.

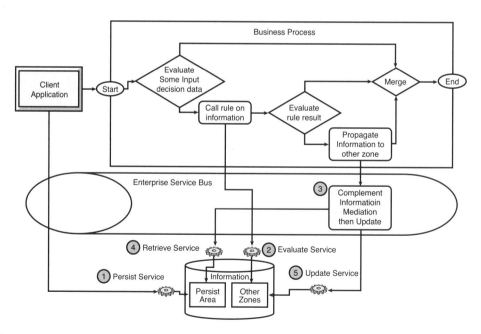

Figure 5-15   Separation of decisional data from persistence bulk

In Figure 5-15, the client application calls the Persist Service (1) first and then passes to the process only the subset that the process needs. Then in the bottom flow, some additional evaluation is required of the Evaluate Service (2), which returns the result of this data analysis. Then if that information needs to be propagated to another zone in the information space the process calls the Enterprise Services Bus, which applies a mediation (3) that uses the Retrieve Service (4) to complement the messages required by the Update Service (5). Using this approach additional data can be added without affecting the process. An additional improvement can be to use mediation between the application and the process so that the application does not perform the separation anymore but instead a bus mediation separates the data for persistence from the data for the process.

A secondary benefit of limiting the amount of data that flows through process choreography engines is that most of these engines' performance is affected by the size of the data, particularly for long-running processes requiring persistence of that information in an underlying database.

Many of the BPEL engines use JDBC to persist the process data and VARCHAR variable character strings. As soon as the VARCHAR or TABLESPACE limit is crossed (this limit depends on the database provider), some of the engines switch to a mode that may impact severely the performance. Overall, containing the process data to the smallest possible size has functional and nonfunctional benefits toward more agility and variability.

Realizing Event Driven Business Processes

A dynamic approach to the implementation of processes is to consider the processes a chain of events triggering some components with actions implementing business logic. In turn, that logic generates events but neither expects nor waits for the results of these events. The result is that the end-to-end process is realized implicitly by this chain, and a given logic in the chain does not need to know what the next step is. This gives a modular approach to processes where a new event listener can be addressed to the process chain without affecting any on the event issuers.

The true difference in an event driven approach is that pure event driven approaches are opportunistic while services approaches are deterministic. This means that if the issuer of the event message expects a specific action as a consequence of this event this is a strict service oriented architecture (SOA) interaction with a deterministic approach and not an event driven dynamic approach.

On the contrary, if the issuer of the message does not expect a specific action as the result of the event message, but if listeners examine the message and apply some rules to make out if they have to do something about it, then we are in a true event driven architecture (EDA).

After the listener has made out that it matches the condition that requires him to handle that event, it will, however, call services that can be the façade to private processes. The deterministic and nondeterministic approaches can complement themselves as business processes can be triggered by events, and asynchronous services can be considered events triggering an action. So in essence, there is not such a big difference between an event driven approach and an asynchronous services approach. In addition, standards such as WS-Notification and WS-BPEL include all the necessary support for managing correlation of incoming events and instances of processes.

Some standards try to address that integration between event driven and services oriented architecture. An example of this continuity between the event approach and the services approach is the telecommunication industry Multi-Technology Operations System Interface (MTOSI) standard that identifies message exchange patterns and communication styles in its MTOSI XML Implementation User Guide: MSG (message) and RPC (remote procedure call) describing the interaction mode.

The message mode in Table 5-2 can be considered an event mode. As shown in Table 5-2, concrete approaches try to use both approaches where they make sense.

Table 5-2   Message Exchange Patterns Supported in MTOSI V1.0[3]

	Communication Pattern			
Communication Style	Simple Response	Multiple Batch Response	File Bulk Response	Notification
MSG (Asynchronous)	(ARR) Asynchronous Request/Reply	(ABR) Asynchronous Batch Response	(AFB) Asynchronous (File) Bulk	(AN) Notification with async subscription
RPC (Synchronous)	(SRR) Synchronous Request/Reply	(SIT) Synchronous Iterator	(SFB) Synchronous File Bulk	(SN) Notification with sync subscription

An implication of this dynamic and modular event driven process approach is that there is no concrete process model. The end-to-end representation of event driven processes is a pure abstract representation, as no formal executable script is expected from the representation of the process. However, business monitoring requires the construction of the implicit process. This representation provides a selective view of the chain of events that happened between the initial event and the last action.

This is typically the way that we address the abstract process monitoring in Chapter 8, "Managing and Monitoring a Dynamic BPM and SOA Environment."

Summary

In this chapter, we saw that dynamic and flexible processes require first an appropriate design for a modularity approach aligned with the enterprise business architecture. We defined rules for modularizing processes and having appropriate services granularity. I want to reinforce, at this stage, that a manageable private process has only one business owner and should focus on a main core entity. This does not imply at all that the end-to-end process does not exist, but just that it is composed by a chain of private processes tied together by services that end up being the contracts between business owners.

Then we looked at ensuring an implementation structure that optimizes the service life cycle, packaging the services interfaces into an idealized application map structure. This was followed by means to extract the logic from processes in business rules and semantic enabled mediation layers. Finally, we discussed event driven approaches and the implication on monitoring. Chapter 8 shows how the end-to-end process view and monitoring can still exist without requiring a matching end-to-end explicit choreography.

Another aspect that we addressed was limiting the impact of information changes to process life cycle and ways of making process behavior more generic so that they could become data content driven and policy driven. As always, in best practices, there are cases where architectural decisions lead to different process implementation choices. The only essential recommendation is that these choices have to be clearly documented and the impact well analyzed so that maintenance and subsequent evolutions are done with a perfect as is knowledge.

In conclusion, I choose to borrow the term KISS, or Keep It Simple and Solid. I can't say it any better: Keep your processes simple and stable.

CHAPTER 6

Implementing the Enterprise Expansion Joint

"Your compassion," answered the shrub, "arises from a kind nature; but leave off this care. The winds are less fearful to me than to you. I bend and do not break."

The Oak and the Reed *by Jean de La Fontaine (translation by Eli Siegel)*

An Enterprise Expansion Joint for Flexible Integration

The term **enterprise expansion joint** is appropriate in that flexible enterprise integration often requires more than a simple stateless Enterprise Services Bus (ESB) mediating the input and output of services interactions. A reusable and flexible services layer applying the granularity practices described in previous chapters potentially requires additional handling and adaptation to match the interfaces exposed by the provider applications.

The need for more complex integration and matchmaking has led to divergent views on the functions an Enterprise Service Bus should contain, particularly whether process and workflow engines should be a part of a bus. Architecture is largely about separation of concerns. As an architect, I am separating what relates to IT-owned service interactions, short-lived, rather stateless interactions, from what are longer business owned interactions and enterprise processes. Therefore, in the following discussion, I use the IBM definition of an Enterprise Services Bus, which defines four primary responsibilities:

- The first responsibility of a bus is the routing of messages resulting from service interactions. Rather than the service requestor calling the service provider directly, the requestor sends a request to the ESB, and the ESB is then responsible for making the call on the service provider.

- Second, the ESB is responsible for converting transport protocols. If the service requestor called directly to the service provider, they would need to use the same transport protocol. The ESB enables the service requestor to use one transport protocol while the service provider uses another.

- Third, the ESB is responsible for transforming message formats. By eliminating the direct call from the service requestor to the service provider, the ESB can modify the message so that the interfaces used by the requestor and provider do not have to be identical.

- Finally, the ESB is capable of handling business events from disparate sources. Therefore, the same service provider responsible for performing some particular business function can be indirectly invoked from a variety of application contexts.

The sources a bus accesses are exposed as services or through adapters. Adapters are designed to help turn existing applications and other application assets into SOA-compliant components, using Java, SCA, or Web Services standards. Thus, these applications are made accessible to the buses in both directions, from and to the applications. The SCA organization defines a binding for Java Connector Architecture.[1] Given these capabilities, most of the existing enterprise information systems can be exposed as SOA components, but this does not imply that the appropriate reusable granularity interfaces are readily available.

The need for dynamicity, granularity adaptation, matchmaking, and semantic functions is a recognized requirement, and these functions are now provided by the integration of buses and their functional extensions in single stacks.[2]

Another industry trend is the federation of buses and integration functions.[3] Experience shows that because of specific needs, enterprises have implemented multiple technologies that perform service integration functions. Because exposing services on the Internet is a new access point for security threats, appliances with a service routing function are dedicated to high throughput XML security and content validation,[4] with choking of invalid services requests. Enterprises or departments with a pure Web Services and Java Enterprise strategic direction look for their internal requirements buses to be based on pure JAX-WS and JMS implementations. Finally, enterprises or lines of business with a history of legacy and mainframe applications have been using buses that also incorporated enterprise application integration and adapter functionalities, and could directly reach the existing applications using their communication protocols.

In Chapter 1, "From Simplified Integration to Dynamic Processes," and Chapter 2, "Streamlining the Enterprise Architecture for Dynamic BPM and SOA," we described a decomposition approach that led to a layer of reusable business services. We also described a granularity adaptation layer that is a purely machine driven layer that exposes the identified reusable, variable, and flexible services to the upper layers and from existing interfaces that preexist and do not have the required granularity and variability.

This layer is what we address now.

Dynamic Adaptation with Enterprise Service Buses

The SOA infrastructure and particularly the ESBs have evolved toward more runtime flexibility. They use policies, mediation flows, message flows, message rule flows, or a combination of all of these.

Mediation flows, message flows, or rules flows use configurable and programmable elements to intercept and modify messages that are passed between existing services (providers) and clients (requesters) that want to use those services (the name of the flow varies by implementation).

Policies address different control domains and purposes. They can define access control in an externalized format, usually in XML. These policies may, for example, specify directives that require message security with digital signing for all messages and authorization control; they can also address service-level agreement definitions, such as specifying that platinum customer services levels must comply to a response time under a given threshold, or that platinum customers access preferred services.

Mediation Flows, Message Flows, Rules Flows

The mediation flows consist of sequences of processing steps called mediations, rules actions, or flow nodes that are executed when a service message is handled through the bus. These mediations, actions, or nodes receive a service interaction message; apply transformations, data handling, or policies; and then make a decision on what the next primitive or node in the flow should be.

Mediation flows or rules can be fast and usually perform simpler actions, such as with WebSphere DataPower® appliances with validation of XML schemas and security. Figure 6-1 shows a DataPower message flow rule editor.

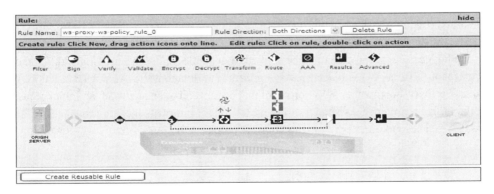

Figure 6-1 DataPower message flow rule editor

There can also be more complexity in an environment supporting more mediation capabilities, including Java custom code mediation support.

Figure 6-2 shows a mediation flow where two implementations of the service use logging and a database lookup to find additional information on the customer requesting the service and then perform the endpoint selection based on the resulting customer level. The filter mediation applies options to identify whether the customer has an appropriate level to be served with a real-time stock quote.

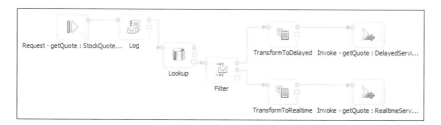

Figure 6-2   WebSphere Integration Developer StockQuote service example

The limit of this example is that the routing is predefined by the mediation flow logic. By integrating policies from a service registry, the flow logic in Figure 6-2 can become much more dynamic.

Dynamic Routing

Variability and coarser granularity of services lead to multiple service implementations for the same interface. Business service consumers can be any channel or process and have to be bound with one of the various implementations, based on policies without embedding the endpoint selection in the client logic. This endpoint selection responsibility now lies with the ESB accessing the registry, which stores the policy definitions. There are two main ways of performing dynamic selection: node-based routing or using a dedicated policy engine to perform the dynamic assembly of the interface with the endpoint.

In both cases, special care must be applied to dynamic routing when using additional control protocols, such as WS-ReliableMessaging, WS-Coordination, WS-AtomicTransaction, WS-BusinessActivity, or any other WS-* protocol that occurs end to end between an initial requester and the ultimate provider. As shown in Figure 6-3, these protocols include sequences of XML messages that need to occur between the same endpoints.

```
<wsrm:Sequence ...>
        <wsu:Identifier> [URI] </wsu:Identifier>
        <wsrm:MessageNumber> [unsignedLong]
        </wsrm:MessageNumber>
        <wsrm:LastMessage/>
        <wsu:Expires> [dateTime] </wsu:Expires>
</wsrm:Sequence>
```

Figure 6-3   Sequence template with message number in a reliable messaging exchange

Thus, after an initial endpoint has been selected, all subsequent interactions for that particular service must occur between the services consumer and the same endpoint.

Node-Based Routing

The Endpoint Lookup mediation or Node is a primitive that sends queries to the registry, retrieves a selection of potential endpoints, and then dynamically routes service messages to the appropriate endpoints based on criteria defined by the mediation, message flow, or rule flow developer.

In all the IBM buses, the endpoint lookup searches for service information within a Web-Sphere Service Registry and Repository (WSRR). The service endpoint information can relate directly to Web Services or to Service Component Architecture (SCA) module exports.

To use the Endpoint Lookup mediation primitive, you might need to add service endpoint information to your registry. If you want to extract service endpoint information about Web Services, your registry must contain either the appropriate WSDL documents or SCA modules that contain exports using Web Service bindings. If you want to extract service endpoint information about exports that use the default SCA binding, your registry must contain the appropriate SCA modules. The endpoint lookup node is inserted in the flow where the dynamic routing is required as shown in Figure 6-4.

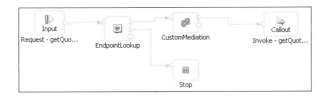

Figure 6-4   Dynamic endpoint selection

As more than one endpoint might be returned, a subsequent mediation is required to set the selected destination. This mediation selects a single service endpoint from the returned reference list and places it in the target address element of the service message object header.

Policy Driven Dynamic Assembly

At runtime, the mediation engine uses service interaction characteristics either from the message itself or from the usage context to find the best suited endpoint or service realization for a consumer based on their business requirements. Characteristics describe the capabilities of an endpoint and can be along any of the dimensions, including Performance, Reliability, Interoperability, Security, and Manageability. Figure 6-5 is an example that attaches an account size to the selection of the endpoint.

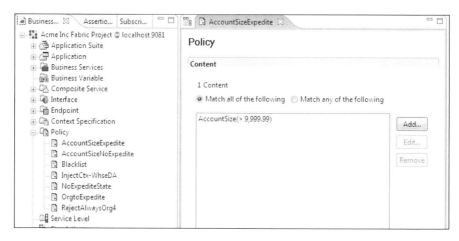

Figure 6-5   Example of routing assertion in a policy

In the IBM metamodel, these business requirements are called policies. A **policy** consists of three sections: The first section is the context of the service request that contains the incoming channel information, including security and roles. The second section is the request itself with the message and the extract semantic elements from the message. Finally, the last section of the policy contains the requirements that must be met, modeled as assertions to form a chain leading to the endpoint selection. These requirements can be either related to the source of the request, some semantic information content in the message such as a product category, or a service level.

Assertions can be attached to endpoints to specify a particular characteristic of an endpoint; for example, an assertion can specify the maximum transaction time available from an endpoint. The contract portion of a policy specifies the collection of assertions that apply to a particular business service content or context. During runtime, if the business service has an applicable policy, then the policy contract is applied. When the policy is fired, the contract is applied; if target, context, and content conditions are satisfied, then the contract is enforced.

With its WebSphere Business Service Fabric product,[5] IBM provides an optimized semantic extension to enterprise service buses that can interpret such policies captured as Web Ontology Language (OWL)[6] format. This extension has a runtime engine called the IBM Business Services Dynamic Assembler that is the access point to services requests and performs dynamic routing.

Relevant policies retrieved from the services registry where they are stored are executed at runtime by the IBM Business Services Dynamic Assembler, which dynamically selects the most appropriate endpoint based on the policies. The semantic mediation engine is highly scalable and is comparable in performance to what customer programming would provide using policy-based composition and semantic mediation for dynamic service assembly and service behavior adaptation based on content, context, and contract.

Creating Routing Context and Adding Business Semantics in Bus Mediations

The dynamic routing described previously requires a context injector to intercept and analyze the messages to then construct the information necessary to find the appropriate endpoints. However, additional business rules may be needed to perform that analysis. For example, determining whether a customer is bronze, silver, or gold may require the application of some business semantics contained in business rules such the ones described in Chapter 5, "Implementing Dynamic Business Processes."

It is possible and even simple to add an external rules engine as an additional filter. A well-known business rules engine on the market is ILog JRules,[7] so Figure 6-6 uses the ILog rules engine's APIs.

```
import ilog.rules.res.model.IlrPath;
import ilog.rules.res.session.IlrJ2SESessionFactory;
import ilog.rules.res.session.IlrSessionCreationException;
import ilog.rules.res.session.IlrSessionRequest;
import ilog.rules.res.session.IlrSessionResponse;
import ilog.rules.res.session.IlrStatelessSession;
import com.webify.fabric.engine.extension;
import com.ibm.fabrictorules.SerializableEndpointList;
public class rulesEndpointFilter implements interface EndpointFilter {
public void filterCandidates(EndPointList endpointList) {
  // SerializableEndpointList is a customer class not described that
makes
  // sure that a remote engine can also handle Fabric endpoint lists
  SerializableEndpointList sEndpointList=
      new SerializableEndpointList(endpointList);
  IlrJ2SESessionFactory factory = new IlrJ2SESessionFactory();
  // Create a new ILog session request object
  IlrSessionRequest sessionRequest = factory.createRequest();
  sessionRequest.setRulesetPath(IlrPath.parsePath(
      "fabricRoutingRuleApp/fabricRoutingRules"));
  // … Set the input parameters for the execution of the rules
  Map inputParameters = new HashMap();
  parameters.put("endpointList", sEndpointList);
  sessionRequest.setInputParameters(inputParameters);
  try {
      // Create the stateless rule session.
      session = factory.createStatelessSession();
      // Execute rules
      IlrSessionResponse sessionResponse =
session.execute(sessionRequest);
      // sEndPointList is an IN_OUT parameter,
      // so can be modified by the rule engine
      // Feedback to WebSphere Fabric Engine
      sresult.setRejectedEndpoints(endPointList);
    } catch (Exception e) { }
  }
}
```

Figure 6-6   Sample code to bridge between dynamic assembler and ILog JRules using JSR94

WebSphere Fabric provides the com.webify.fabric.engine.extension.EndpointFilter interface to expose external filtering engines.

Using the example in Figure 6-6, integration enterprises can then manage all business rules from a single rules engine point of control. The ILog rules engine interfaces or JSR-94 rules engines interfaces[8] can also be used in more classical ESB mediation flows. The Java JSR-94 is an old JSR that defines a standardized rules engine's APIs; however, it never made its way into J2EE.

Managing State

In exposing the required service interfaces from existing services, some data may not be exposed on the interface or may be provided on the incoming request and not be defined and used by the target application interface but rather revived on the response.

An example of this state preservation is the evolution between the various releases of financial messages where a new mandatory field appeared in Settlement Instructions and Confirmations messages defined by the international financial message SWIFT organization. This affected message types MT540 through MT547. Thus during a transition phase, existing systems needed to store the incoming data, perform some message transformation to map to old formats, call the old systems, and on the way back restore the preserved information on the responses.

There are many other examples of such requirements for state preservation in layers that primarily were designed for stateless interactions.

Using Database to Preserve State

An immediate thought for state preservation is to use database mediations to preserve data flowing through the buses. These mediations can update a database from information coming from a message. The database mediations can also add to, or change, messages using information from a user-supplied database and then the updated message are propagated. Finally, these mediations can delete elements from databases.

However, a concern is to avoid indefinite expansion of tables, and to ensure cleanup occurs after state has been revived and state became useless. In addition to the correlation key, a state should then always be stored with additional context information, such as time stamps or service identifiers. The context information allows then safe batch cleanups of the state tables. In addition, the database access can cause performance problems.

Using Message Queuing (MQ) to Preserve State

Given that each service interaction has exactly one response per request, a message queue can be used to store the state information as a message while the service provider processes the requests. This requires the use of message correlation information that must be present in the request message and in the responses.

When this approach is feasible, it improves the state preservation performance dramatically.

Structured Hierarchical Contexts

Servlet programmers are familiar with the Servlet context where they store Web Session related data. Structured contexts consist in multiple similar data storage areas chained together to form a tree representation, where a lower leaf of the tree can preserve data for a particular interaction only, while the upper leaves maintain longer-lived information.

The implementation of structured context is either a local or remote tree container accessible with keys. These contexts are global hierarchical data space defined as collections, fully customizable, with dynamic management of context nodes. The data is accessible by name and externally defined, and a context data is shared among all of its subcontexts. Any structured data element in the collections can contain simple or complex data elements. These context trees usually contain transient information in the lower branches, but also longer persistent information in the higher branches. For contextual information that must be preserved for longer periods, the Enterprise Java Beans (EJB) instances create and maintain the server side of remote contexts.

This is the model used by the IBM WebSphere Multichannel Branch Transformation Toolkit (BTT), and the BTT Context tree is a central piece of the framework (see Figure 6-7). Contexts in BTT are chained in a hierarchical way, according to the business organization, from general to specific (for example, from branch to workstation to operation).

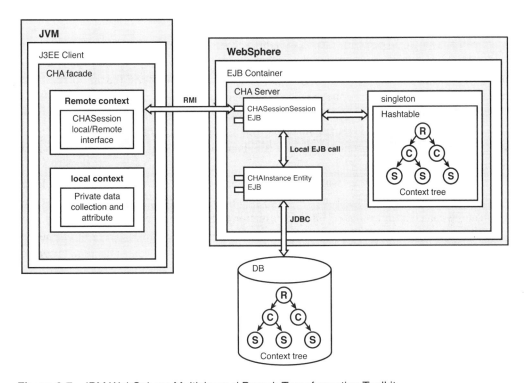

Figure 6-7   IBM WebSphere Multichannel Branch Transformation Toolkit

Requests to the contexts structure for data and services are handled in a way that allows the resources to be placed in the context chain in the best position for the requirements. The name of an information resource must be unique within a single context, but it does not have to be unique in the scope of the context hierarchy. The same name can be used for a data resource in different contexts, and the search path to locate the resource can be followed up to the root context (the one with no parent). However, the data that is returned will be located in the closest context level structure from where the search was initiated.

Work Area Service for J2EE

The need to preserve states in a distributed computing environment includes the ability to pass that information from one component to another. However, that information is not always exposed by the component interfaces. For example, middleware services propagate that information implicitly in addition to the arguments passed in remote requests. Typically, security certificates and transaction contexts are passed implicitly. Developers do not have to code that information in the method interfaces, which lessens the use of the corresponding services. This information is carried implicitly by the environment based on some common context, which can be the current thread or the current transaction.

Within a single process, Java provides a thread local memory ThreadLocal<T> that allows for the storage of a data instance that then becomes accessible from every request within the same thread without passing that data explicitly.[9] However, ThreadLocal provides thread isolated information and cannot pass that information along to remote methods.

The WebSphere work area service[10] is a J2EE extension that passes information explicitly as an argument or implicitly to remote methods. You can define bidirectional or nonbidirectional work area partitions. If the partition is defined as bidirectional, the context propagates from a target object back to the originator.

Developers set properties within a thread of an application context that are implicitly attached to processing and made available at any point during the processing of remote requests. Applications can create a work area, insert information into it, and make remote invocations. That work area information is then propagated with each remote method invocation. This eliminates the need to explicitly include the arguments in the method definitions, enable the remote components to use, or update that data and have the requesters access this modified data.

If methods in a server receive a work area from a client and subsequently invoke other remote methods, the work area is transparently propagated with the remote requests. When the creating application is done with the work area, it terminates it. There is no restriction on the data types that work areas can hold; however, reasonable sizes of data should be passed using work areas.

The information in a work area includes a set of properties consisting of **key-value-mode** triplets. The key-value-mode triplets represent the information contained in the property; the key is a name by which the associated value is retrieved. The mode determines whether you can modify or remove the property. A simple rewriting of the information of a property in a work area modifies its value. Using work area nesting applications, specific scopes can be defined to contain properties for specific tasks without making the work areas available to all parts of the application. As shown in Figure 6-8, a nested work area's temporary override of a property with a given key does not affect the containing work area, if that property key has been defined in the nested area.

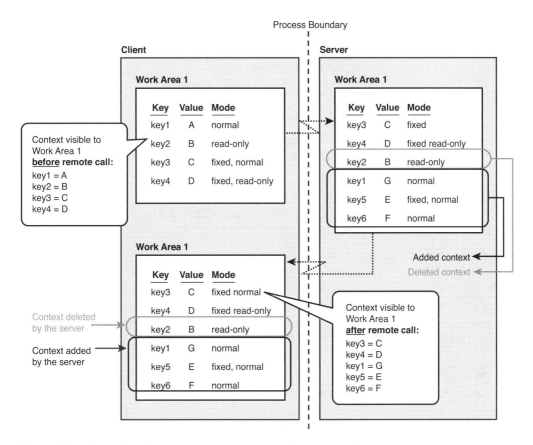

Figure 6-8   Example client and server work area with nested work area

By default, on each set operation the attribute set into a work area is automatically serialized by the work area service. On each subsequent get operation on that same attribute, it is deserialized and returned to the requester. Excessive serialization and deserialization can result in observable performance degradation under a heavy load, and deferred attribute serialization configuration property is a caching feature that reduces serialization and deserialization operations. Then attributes are not actually serialized until the thread with which the attribute is associated makes a remote IIOP invocation. Just as with ThreadLocal, work areas must be used cautiously in applications that use threading as work areas started on one thread are not available on another unless there is a remote method interaction between these threads.

A UserWorkArea partition is defined from the configuration interface, and a corresponding JNDI naming is defined such as java:comp/websphere/UserWorkArea, as shown in Figure 6-9. Applications that need to access their partition can perform a lookup on that JNDI name.

```
import com.ibm.websphere.workarea.*;
import javax.naming.*;
public class SimpleSampleServlet {
  ...
  InitialContext jndi = null;
  UserWorkArea userWorkArea = null;
  try {
      jndi = new InitialContext();
      userWorkArea = (UserWorkArea)jndi.lookup(
"java:comp/websphere/UserWorkArea");
      ...

      userWorkArea.set(key,value);

  }
catch (NamingException e) { ... }}
```

Figure 6-9   Example work area code

Techniques for Mediating Service for Variability and Granularity Aggregation

Services exposed from existing Enterprise Information Systems or commercial packages rarely expose implementation independent interfaces. With the required granularity and variability of the information model, we need for the integration layer to provide such aggregation and variability to less variable integration. The techniques range from a simple fan out to services and fan in of the response, to more complex and short-lived flows that integrate systems with conditional decisions within the flows.

Fan Out/Fan In

You can use the Fan Out and Fan In mediation primitives to aggregate the responses from two services or more invocations into one output message.

Using WebSphere ESB for Aggregation

The first process is a mediation flow for WebSphere Enterprise Service Bus that directly links the two services. Each one is called synchronously in its branch and then aggregates the result. We could also imagine the separation the fan out invokes from the fan (shown in Figure 6-10), as described in the "Building an Aggregation Function Using WebSphere ESB" developerWorks® article.[11]

Figure 6-10   Fan Out and Fan In WebSphere Integration Developer

There is a shared context area for storing aggregation data in a thread-based storage area, so it can be used to transmit information between a Fan Out primitive and a Fan In primitive, but only if they are defined in the same flow. The content of the shared context will be lost across a request flow and a response flow through callout invocation. As the response will be in a separate thread, the fan out data will be lost if not aggregating in the same flow.

Libraries of XLST mediation primitives should be built to map each generic service message input or output to and from whatever the target services interfaces expose.

Using WebSphere Message Broker for Aggregation

In messaging-oriented middleware (MOM) environments (based on IBM WebSphere MQ [WMQ]) that integrate directly with an enterprise transactional system, such as IBM's WebSphere IMS™ or WebSphere CICS, WebSphere Message Broker is often the preferred choice of ESB. It usually is the preferred choice because it can reach these systems directly using the provided output and input nodes for MQ, IMS interactions with the IMSRequest node, or the CICSRequest public supportpac if you are using Message Broker from a z/OS® environment.12 In that case, the fan out and fan in can be developed as message flows.

There are three nodes for controlling the fan out and fan in, as shown in Figure 6-11:

- **AggregateControl**—Marks the beginning of a fan out of requests that are part of an aggregation
- **AggregateRequest**—Records the fact that request messages have been sent
- **AggregateReply**—Marks the end of an aggregation fan-in and collects the replies to combine them

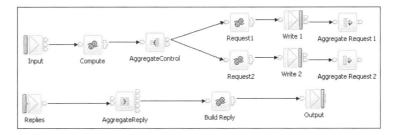

Figure 6-11   WebSphere Message Broker fan out and fan in

Also note that aggregation nodes in WebSphere Message Broker Version 6 can use a set of WMQ queues, instead of writing this data to the database. Thus the message flow can be made nonpersistent, and this improves performance and throughput, as there is no more database access overhead.

Using WebSphere DataPower for Fan Out and Fan In Aggregation

WebSphere DataPower can also be used for fan out and fan in aggregations. The difficult part of the implementation is the fan in step. To implement this aggregation pattern in the WebSphere DataPower appliance family (firmware versions 3.6.1 and later), the following steps are required:

1. In the main rule, create a for-each action configured to use an XPath iterator that handles the fan out and that uses for its target action, the named rule defined as follows.

    This name rule handles each of the branches you need to create a named processing rule with a sequence of actions, or a "transform," for the XSLT transformation using INPUT as its input, a "results" to perform the input mapping, and another "transform" for the Web Service result XSLT transformation then using OUTPUT as the output.

2. The Processing Control File field should specify a variable from the context in the form of var://context/transformin and var://context/transformout that is set to the style sheets to be used for each of the transformations. You can use the DataPower XSLT extension `dp:variable('var://service/multistep/loop-count')` to find the current index in the loop, and `dp:variable('var://service/multistep/loop-iterator')` gets the current node.

3. Then after the for-each action, another "transform" action needs to be performed that consolidates all the results from each of the services using each `dp:variable('var://context/loopout_n/')` to get the result tree from each iteration (where "n" is the branch index).

WS-BPEL Micro-Flows

In some cases, the flow logic available from ESB mediations, such as fan out or fan in, are not sufficient to address all the aggregation requirements, for instance, maintaining keys relationships. Some enterprises may define a governance principle that states all that relates to flows should use the same standardized WS-BPEL representation. However, for such aggregation flows, we need short-lived, nonpersistent mode. WS-BPEL only addresses the execution semantics of the business logic. The runtime aspects are left to the implementers.

IBM adds specific differentiation, in the business process choreographer of WebSphere Process Server between micro-flows and long-running flows, and these differences are detailed in Table 6-1. But let me emphasize the micro-flows that we focus on here for aggregation purposes.

A micro-flow is uninterruptible and runs in one physical thread from start to finish. They are sometimes referred to as noninterruptible business processes. A micro-flow uses the WS-BPEL standard and in IBM technology, uses the WebSphere Process Server as the engine. However, as it is noninterruptible it cannot contain human tasks, or any wait activities, implying that child processes should also be micro-flows. Because the micro-flow is transient it does not require any persistence, and the performance is usually very good. For example, we use this type of micro-flow in a large telco environment with hundreds of parallel flows taking less than 100ms. A micro-flow may run in an atomic transaction.

The attributes for micro-flows and long-running business processes as defined by the WebSphere Process Server are summarized in Table 6-1.

Table 6-1 Attributes for Micro-Flows and Long-Running Business Processes

Process Type	Micro-Flow	Long-Running Business Process
Transactions	One transaction for the entire process.	Transaction boundaries can be set between each activity.
Persistence	None.	Processes can be persisted to a database and restarted.
Crash Recovery	None, execution is completely transient; state is kept in RAM.	Process can resume from the last checkpoint.
Parallelism	None, strictly single-threaded, micro-flow parallelism is only in the model; in reality, branches are executed in sequence. Deadlocks can occur if not designed carefully.	Flow activities can run in parallel
Interruptible	No.	Yes.
Interruptible	No.	Yes.
Process Correlation Support	No	Yes, responses from asynchronous services use correlation sets as defined by BPEL.

Typically, micro-flows are used for maintaining and synchronizing information across systems that use that information. Propagating contract information throughout the organization would use a micro-flow.

Data persistence from a micro-flow, such as the use of an audit log to capture the state of a micro-flow instance, can affect the performance. A message queuing option should be used instead for audit purposes. The services integrated from a micro-flow running inside a transaction boundary defined in that flow participate in the micro-flow transaction; those outside the boundary do not participate in the transaction.

Managing Granularity from Mainframe with CICS Service Flow Modeler

The CICS transaction server is used by the majority of the world's financial sector as well as other enterprises in various industries. A huge amount of existing logic is written in COBOL and CICS that is worth reusing. However, the granularity of the existing transactions rarely matches

the consumer need, and many of the existing transactions are developed as 3270 terminal applications (so-called green screens).

Screen scraping and wrapping these transactions with an emulator does not always provide
the support for transaction control and performance that is required for a scalable SOA integration. In CICS implementation evolutions, the new applications have been using a more service-
orientated approach because the distributed program link (DPL) is used, which exposes CICS
business logic as input and output communication areas, in many cases accessed with MQ.
Recently, the support for Web Services was added. The result is that enterprises may have any of
the preceding logic and need to integrate them into a single service.

The CICS Service Flow Feature provides the capability to aggregate existing CICS applications into composed business services that can be integrated into an SOA environment. It is a
business service integration adapter for all CICS applications. There are two main capabilities
within the CICS service flow feature:

1. Automate the interaction with 3270 terminal based applications, create from it a link-
    able service, and expose it as a business level service.

2. Aggregate multiple calls to CICS applications in one single aggregated application to
    external clients as a business level service call. You can turn fine-grained CICS applica-
    tions into the required coarse-grained business services.

Just like the BPEL micro-flows, a service flow is a noninterruptible micro-flow that is constructed
from a collection of nodes that represent the invocation of CICS resources:

• The flow describes the navigation of the nodes and allows data mapping between the
   nodes.

• A single request may cause the execution of many CICS resources.

• Allows for the development of coarse-grained services from fine-grained resources.

Figure 6-12 is a simple example of the Service Flow Modeler visual tool.

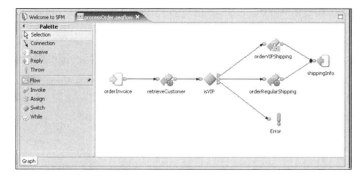

Figure 6-12   Service Flow Modeler sample flow

The Service Flow Modeler can integrate various components in service flows using three categories of nodes: 1) input and output, 2) invoke, and 3) flow control. These nodes are the following:

- **While**—Flow control loop node
- **Switch**—Flow control decision node
- **Assign**—Map data between messages in the flow
- **Invoke Flow**—Invoke a flow
- **Invoke Terminal**—Invoke a terminal screen operation
- **Invoke Operation**—Invoke a nonterminal operation
- **Invoke Generic**—Invoke target not yet defined
- **Throw**—Raising fault node
- **Reply**—Output node from flow
- **Receive**—Input node for flow

The internal model for a flow is based on WSDL and XML schemas, these being automatically mapped to the target transactions or screens. The flow then generates code that is deployed as a CICS TS v3.1 host.

That generated code can then access runtime services provided by CICS that allow it to

- Link to existing CICS applications
- Control terminal based applications via the Link3270 bridge or FEPI (Link3270 has better performance.)
- Call external Web Service via the EXEC CICS INVOKE WEBSERVICE API
- Model PUT/GET pairs with WebSphere MQ

The flows are then exposed as an existing CICS application and can be accessed using the CICS 3.1 access modes, which are

- Linking from another CICS application
- Asynchronous interactions via WebSphere MQ over the CICS/MQ bridge
- Using the JCA client provided with the CICS Transaction Gateway
- Calling as from a Web Service client using the standard CICS Web Services support (support provided out of the box by CICS 3.1)

Split Model Techniques

When a generic service model is defined and exposed, it becomes a pivot canonical model that limits integration costs. This canonical is a well-known concept that has been the base for reducing the mapping requirements since the Enterprise Application Integration (EAI) concept and middleware were introduced.

However, in a more complex environment with multiple sources, the mapping of one aggregation can be cumbersome. Several techniques are available to reduce the implementation cost by creating additional mapping reusability opportunities and more automated resolution of the mapping. These techniques all include the definition of one or more transient information models that expose the interface messages as views from the model. The models have some form of controller that feeds the model from sources.

Single Pivot Object Oriented Information Model

A first implementation is to have the complete information models implemented as a transient model. The model can either be a domain UML model transformed into a concrete runtime model or an equivalent XML schema transformed into a runtime model.

In the first part of the approach, as shown in Figure 6-13, all potential feeds from sources to the model are defined, linking elements in the model to the sources and defining how the mapping occurs for each of these sources.

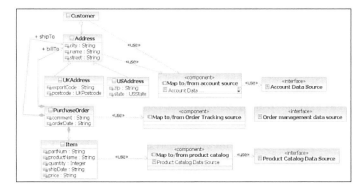

Figure 6-13   Linking model classes to data sources with maps

The next part, as shown in Figure 6-14, is to define what we want to expose as an interface from the model, not caring about how the graph resolves the connections to the data sources.

«message» PurchaseOrderRequestMessage	- purchaseOrderRequest	PurchaseOrder comment : String orderDate : String

Figure 6-14   Linking messages to model

The trick here is to have an implementation that can identify the model graph that a particular message needs. The data sources then are implicitly triggered by the implied object classes linked to the data sources. The graph resolution needs to be selective and identify only the direct paths to sources so as to avoid pulling all of the sources. In Figure 6-14, the purchase order should not trigger the map between customer and source because there is no direct association from purchase order to customer, but only the opposite. However, particular care must be applied to selecting data sources to avoid multiple paths ending at the same data source interface to be called multiple times.

Using the out of the box UML to Java transformations and appropriate patterns in Rational Software Architect, one can deliver such information model pivot integration with an optimized access to the information source.

A UML-based integration method is also available as a commercial product from some software vendors. In this approach, the consumers of the model only care about the elements they need to expose in their services messages, and they identify these elements in the pivot UML model. The engine then automatically selects the data source feeds linked to the classes used directly or indirectly by relationship in the model and optimize this source access.

Context Tree or Context Area Based Integration

Another approach to the pivot model is to use a context represented as a tree and accessible with keys. This context tree can be implemented as a structure context tree or a work area as described in previous sections of this chapter.

In the intermediate tier, first the service request's messages populate the context tables using the data names as keys to input the context. When a request needs to be propagated to the referenced services, the information is retrieved using the referenced services' request message names. Then, the responses from these services are automatically parsed by name to feed the context. This process is shown is Figure 6-15.

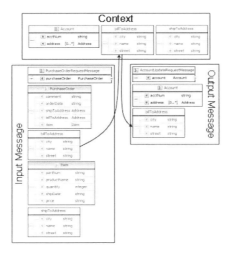

Figure 6-15   Using context as a buffer between input and output messages

At this point, the context behaves as a tamper that absorbs incoming information based on the naming structure defined by the context, for example billToAddress in Figure 6-15, and makes it available on request by name. If the context is implemented with EJBs or a remote area, the buffering of information is allowed for better performance caching information such as a list of accounts for a given customer.

Cascading Model View Controller

The models described in the previous sections do not always represent the reality of the enterprise. Often, there are submodels local to lines of business, or even technical models. These models are a combination of locally managed information and views of the integrated component models, shown in Figure 6-16. In this case, the local context as described in the previous section can become the model for that tier.

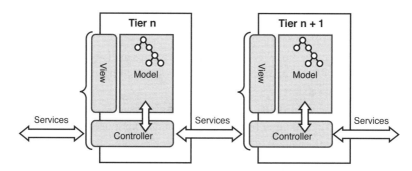

Figure 6-16   Cascade of MVC with services interacting with controllers accessing models

This can be the case where intermediate tiers are used to broker information coming from several other services sources. This model is often the model used by Master Data Management (MDM) systems to aggregate information. The client tier provides in its model a single view of customers, of products, or any enterprise entities from disparate services sources exposing particular models. A local caching is performed by these MDM systems to optimize the access to the synthesized information.

Managing Transactional Units of Works in Granularity Adaptation

When aggregating several interfaces from target systems into one higher granularity, some of these systems require consistency and the use of an atomic transactional control. Because the purpose of an atomic transaction is to coordinate resource managers that isolate transactional updates by holding transactional locks on resources, it is generally not recommended that atomic transactions be distributed across enterprise domains.

You should keep this atomic transaction control as close as possible to the integrated system. Several options are available depending on the way the target systems are accessed:

- Java Connector Architecture adapter exists

- Web Services interface with WS-AtomicTransaction support

- None of the above exists and the system offers APIs for transactional control in another technology

If a Java Connector Architecture compliant adapter exists, with the transactional support exposed as service provider interfaces, this adapter should be used and the transactional context controlled by the bus mediation flows or micro-flows.

If the target system only exposes WS-AtomicTransaction (WS-AT) on a Web Service interface, then this protocol can be used from an application server client. This usually happens with services developed with application servers aggregated from a remote application server behaving as a bus extension.

WS-AT is an XML-based, two-phase commit transaction protocol and is suitable for short duration transactions only. The WebSphere Application Server runtime takes responsibility for the registration of WS-AT participants in the same way as the registration of XA resources (X/Open eXtended Architecture specification for distributed transaction processing) in the Java Transaction API (JTA) transaction to which the WS-AT transaction is federated. At transaction completion time, all XA resources and WS-AT participants are atomically coordinated by the WebSphere Application Server transaction service. If dynamic routing is enabled given that WS-AT is a client to service provider transaction control, no dynamic routing of the WS-AT XML messages to a different target can occur after a first endpoint selection for the aggregated services. It is also important to note that WS-AT is using XML and thus leads to higher data exchange volumes to control of the two-phase commit flows.

If no adapter or WS-AT support exist, or if WS-AT exists but is not a good choice for performance reasons, then the development of an adapter can be a good choice. Adapter frameworks are provided to simplify such new developments. As an example, in one of our projects the development of an adapter to integrate with a billing system using Tuxedo and C API took just one month to complete.

Propagating Faults from Granularity Adaptation

In all cases of variability and granularity adaptation, the faults must also adapt. The consumer view of the error cannot be the propagation of any of the faults coming from the referenced systems. Business faults should be defined with technical header information common to all faults, such as the message, error codes, and identifier attributes, and then a business section understandable by consumers that provides meaningful information about the error. If possible, fault tags in addition to the service interfaces should be enabled automatically.

Summary

We saw in this chapter that the integration layers between consumers and providers of services sometimes require much more complexity than the base functions provided by an enterprise service bus (routing messages between services, converting transport protocols between requester and service, transforming message formats between requester and service, and handling business events from disparate sources). As much as possible, the intermediaries between consumers and providers should contain the propagation of changes between those consumers and providers, by adding the necessary buffering and semantic matchmaking support.

CHAPTER 7

Tooling for Dynamic SOA and BPM Processes

The expectations of life depend upon diligence; the mechanic that would perfect his work must first sharpen his tools.

Confucius

Managing the Architecture Life Cycle

The purpose of this chapter is not to describe a complete enterprise architecture modeling and software development life cycle, but to highlight where in these life cycles tools can help identify and capture flexibility requirements and artifacts. In a model-driven approach for enterprise architecture, the teams participating in the enterprise architecture life cycle need traceability from business, functional, and nonfunctional requirements to the design and implementation, as well formulated as the traceability is from to the deployment and operational models aspect.

Tooling for Requirements, Change Cases, and Context

As variability cannot always be predefined, the modeling needs to start as a classical approach that employs techniques that help identify articulation and variability points. These articulation and variability points derive from an initial identification of requirement variability and particularly define change cases together with use cases.

It is also essential to start with a formal understanding of the business and IT contexts to identify stable and variable aspects. The business aspects are formalized in models, using the various maps described in Chapter 1, "From Simplified Integration to Dynamic Processes," along with descriptions of enterprise capabilities. These context models also focus on the specific zoomed business areas and describe all the surrounding elements of the targeted solution, such as business actors, technologies, and business events.

The functional requirements captured can take the form of use cases, scenarios, and business processes represented in tools with the appropriate decompositions described in Chapter 5, "Implementing Dynamic Business Processes." Change cases are particularly important for our concern because they look at how business and technical environment changes affect the solution. This change or variability analysis is especially important to ensure solution flexibility. Figure 7-1 shows the elements used to construct an enterprise architecture.

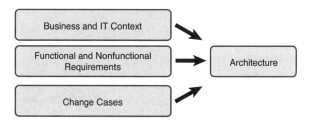

Figure 7-1   Base model elements used to build an architecture

All requirements do not address identical levels of functional decomposition in the enterprise. We then need a differentiation between use cases that happen between lines of business, between business components in a line of business, or lower level use cases.

The common practice is to use business use cases to process higher level requirements and application use cases for what is related to user interaction and lower levels of granularity. In a UML semantic approach, a business process is equivalent to a UML activity diagram and as such is considered to be part of a business use case. However, to differentiate in UML the various levels of requirements captured as use cases, specific UML stereotypes help categorize each of them.

As a source of variability the nonfunctional requirements also need to be formally captured and traced within the models, covering business constraints (for example, 7*24*365), technology constraints (for example, SOAP, WS-I, Linux®), nonruntime qualities (for example, security, manageability, recovery), and runtime qualities (for example, response time, scalability). An example of variability of nonfunctional requirements can be a restriction of operating ranges in certain countries for a company operating internationally.

Traceability is essential, and the tooling must provide support for this traceability between requirements and architecture.

Figure 7-2 is a screen shot of Rational Software Architect for WebSphere showing first the Requirement Explorer window view of the RequisitePro® requirements database, and then the trace between the requirements, and the business use case at the bottom.

As you can see in the Requirements Explorer window in Figure 7-2, you can capture different types of requirement and architectural information. The requirement tool allows you to define the classification that a particular architectural approach needs. Each of the categories listed previously (business goals, key performance indicators, business event, business use cases, business tasks, change cases, nonfunctional requirements, and architectural decisions) has a different template with specific attributes that describe the given category.

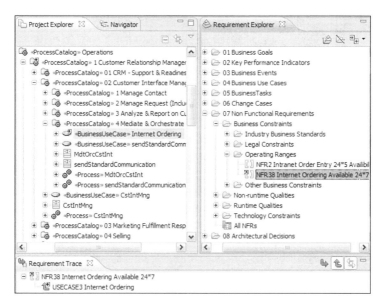

Figure 7-2   Linking requirements and business use cases

For example, each element in a business goals category includes type, priority, status, stability, owner, business benefit, ROI, and cost. For each of the categories, the attributes template generates a specific form, enabling specific reporting and categorization of requirements. The template shown in Figure 7-3 is for architectural decisions, as viewed from Rational Software Architect for WebSphere.

Change cases attempt to look at the future and evaluate the time phase, probability, and impact severity, and then determine the best date to provision for the change. Let me provide a few examples of changes cases here to further clarify. Change cases are unplanned variations of functional or nonfunctional requirements but derive from probable changes of operating conditions. If there is a formal plan to extend the enterprise to identified new channels, this is not a change case, but should be captured as a variation of a use case as the channels are known.

Drivers for change cases are typically regulations, such as tax legislations changing every year or expansion or outsourcing decisions without a specific target yet. These are highly probable, but you cannot anticipate what the change will be. So anything in the enterprise ecosystem that is probable but cannot be precisely defined is a change case.

The first example is a European bank operating in Western Europe that plans to expand to Eastern Europe but has not yet selected the target acquisitions. There is a high probability that the acquired banks will have a different infrastructure and different legislations. These should be considered as two change cases, one purely business for the legislation support, and the second is more technical and involves integrating with whatever core banking application and interfaces are used in the targeted countries.

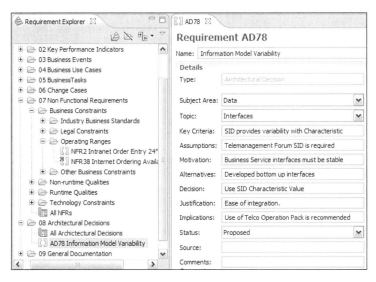

Figure 7-3   Architectural decision template from RequisitePro in RSA

Another typical change case is the foreseeable addition of new reporting requirements, however undefined today, with the use of standard business reporting taxonomies (based on XBRL standard) by the Australian government.[1] Either as an enterprise operating in Australia or as the government itself, you can anticipate that more reports or a different report structure will be required on the reporting services exposed by the government. Identifying these change cases and then tracing them formally to architecture enables the identification of necessary points of variability within the architectural elements.

The business context then enables the identification of external actors and variability derived from the context. Figure 7-4 is an example from a project with a container shipping company that shows many variations, such as for the external booking parties.

Business contexts have to be shared with nontechnical persons, and graphical enhancements make these diagrams easier to communicate. To that purpose, see how pictures can be added to UML stereotypes in specific UMLs used to develop custom profiles, as in the ship image used in Figure 7-4. This allows the UML's use case diagrams to be much more illustrative and presentation friendly, while maintaining the formalism needed and the ability to trace context elements to architectural elements. These images can be any portable network graphic with Rational Software Architect for WebSphere.

The use of UML packaging facilitates the identification of variations categories, and the UML relationship display eases the understanding of the actor categorization. The same actors can then be used in specific use cases to model their interactions with the target system. The approach is first to list all actors, then identify classifications, and finally package by identified categories and subcategories. The approach for actors is exactly the same one used for other variability elements, which is to list, categorize, and create UML packages for the categories.

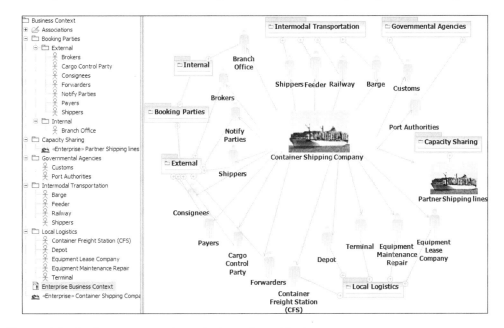

Figure 7-4 Business context of a typical container shipping company

When a set of elements belongs to more than one category, the approach is to create multiple package hierarchies and use the UML package import function to create alternate navigation trees in UML models. We see that approach in more detail when we look at the formalization of multidimensional maps in UML models.

Capturing Enterprise Architecture Models

In Chapter 1, we saw that enterprise architecture differentiates the business, application/services, and infrastructure layers. We now see how tools can capture such maps and layers, enabling the traceability and the transformation that are the basis for model driven architecture approaches.

Enterprise Architecture Tooling Round-Tripping and Direct Deployment

In Chapter 1, we discussed the layering of the enterprise architecture in business, application/services, and information layers. A dynamic environment should enable incremental changes to these layers to be captured from an architectural point of view and propagated to the implementation and deployment in a traceable and accelerated manner.

The metamodel, shown in Figure 7-5, that enables this incremental evolution that we use for capturing these architect models corresponds to the business, application/services, and information layers described in Chapter 1 and uses the relevant categorization within each domain, as already discussed.

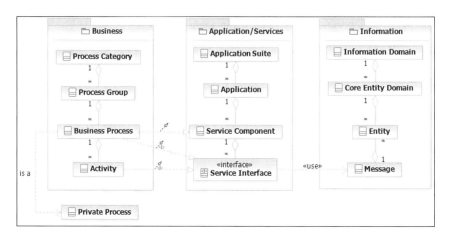

Figure 7-5   Metamodel base for model capture in tooling

The categories for process derive directly from the APQC process classification framework that defines four levels of decomposition: process category classifying business competency domains of the enterprise, process group gathering business components that apply to similar business entities, list of tasks and activities required to achieve a specific aspect of a business component, and activities are the lower level business tasks. The application/services layer is decomposed in application suites that address a particular business domain, and then applications that deliver a set of functions are grouped into services components and interfaces. As previously discussed, information also defines high-level domains decomposed into core entity domains, and entities and sub entities within these domains.

In addition to these three layers, we also look later in this chapter at the deployment aspects with the infrastructure modeling.

But before focusing on each layer modeling in the enterprise architecture domains, let's examine how each of these layers contributes to better control of incremental changes with limitation of the impact of changes and round-tripping. The following approach uses a combination of practice and tools capabilities for this purpose.

One source of incremental change problems is the inconsistency between technical and business domain standards. For example, the BPMN notation standard, the XPDL workflow standard, and the business process execution language WS-BPEL for choreographing services have all been developed by different standardization teams. Consequently, the process model used in the Business Process Management Notation (BPMN) standard has notations that cannot translate directly in either WS-BPEL or XML Process Definition Language (XPDL), without appropriate help from the tooling. This inconsistency if not handled correctly can result in irreversible changes when you transition from the business process model to the technical process model, and these irreversible changes make round-tripping problematic.

Another source of problems is the wide variety of inputs for any given domain. The information modeling industry standards use either UML or XML schemas. For instance, the Common

Information Model (CIM) from the Energy and Utilities standards[2] (available as UML), the Shared Information and Data (SID) model for telcos[3] (available as UML), and the Association for Cooperative Operations Research and Development (ACORD) for insurance[4] (XML models) are all examples of industry standards, but they all use different inputs. As these standards evolve, one has to anticipate versioning problems by consolidation in an intermediate and variable enterprise information model.

So, we use a separation of concerns approach when attempting to deliver round-tripping. First, we consolidate all these information sources into one enterprise consolidated variable information model dedicated to integration purposes. We also consolidate all service identification and packaging into one model and integrate for the specification the messages deriving from the consolidated variable information model. Services and information schemas are stored in the enterprise service registry.

Finally, we derive processes groups from the enterprise decomposition method described previously but then integrate the services and information model from the registry to define the interfaces they expose and the interface they consume.

These junctions become clear identifications of single consolidation points and sources for each business process, service component, and information entity. The consolidation of each domain into a single model includes an impact analysis that helps create the updated consolidation.

Aligned with the metamodel illustrated in Figure 7-5, Figure 7-6 shows the typical approach that looks at optimizing the modeling and implementation.

The business, application/services, and information enterprise architecture layers are represented vertically as in Figure 7-5. The infrastructure as the fourth layer introduced in Chapter 1 is modeled later when looking at the deployment of the elements.

In the IBM environment, the BPMN tool with SOA support is WebSphere Business Modeler, the UML modeling environment with SOA and J2EE implementation is Rational Software Architect for WebSphere, and the tool for integrating SOA components, BPEL business processes, and Service Message mediations is WebSphere Integration Developer. The database related tooling is Rational Data Architect. The infrastructure and deployment modeling also uses Rational Software Architect for WebSphere.

Modeling Business and Application/Services Layers

Now that we looked at the overall process to create the architecture, let's look at the specific layers of the enterprise architecture that are the base for the business, application, and services.

The following sections use many examples from TeleManagement Forum, the standards body that has done the most complete approach in terms of enterprise architecture formal layering. However, all the tooling principles described here are applicable to other industry domains.

When modeling the business maps, we must consider the support of business industry standards such as TeleManagement Forum that are creating multidimensional business maps to categorize their business functions (eTOM).[5] The eTOM map in Chapter 1 consists of vertical and horizontal decompositions into categories that intersect at level 2. The vertical grouping is a direct operation process view, such as fulfillment, assurance, and billing, while the horizontal eTOM are functional process groupings, such as customer relationship management.

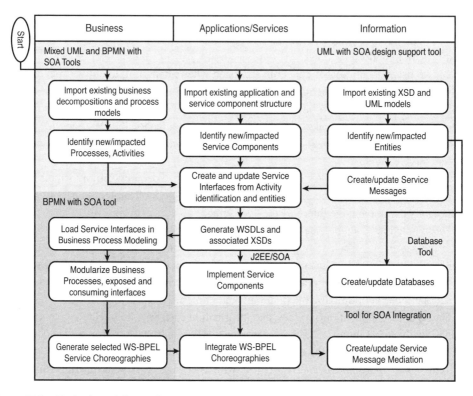

Figure 7-6   Typical modeling to implementation flow for processes, services, and information

These representations as two dimensional maps and particularly the definition of their intersection points are not commonly used in modeling tools, which usually capture tree structures and free layout diagrams. However, with a little additional structure with standard features and some discipline, these representations can be captured.

As shown in Figure 7-7, we start by capturing each category with a packaging of elements that fall into the same semantics. As the intersections are common to both categorization structures the packages that are in the intersection are common to both decompositions.

If we take as an example the business decomposition proposed by eTOM, there is a horizontal decomposition that is customer relationship management (CRM) or service management and operations, the vertical decomposition being fulfillment assurance and billing.

Order Handling is then at the intersection of fulfillment and CRM. As another part of the standard decomposes using the horizontal categories as the base, we create our packaging in UML starting with this same Order Handling tree.

As we have created the eTOM horizontal process functional trees, we now need to create the verticals for the direct operations decomposition of the map. As these verticals only apply to

Figure 7-7   Level 3 process catalog decompositions as UML stereotyped packages

operations for that particular business map, we add these to the operations catalog. Then we use the UML package import to import the packages from the first decomposition. As shown in Figure 7-8, the UML packages are stereotyped as process catalogs.

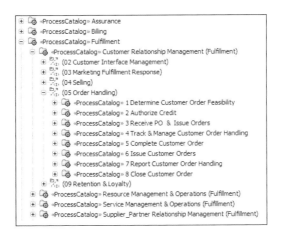

Figure 7-8   Alternate decomposition tree importing selected packages

As you can see from Figure 7-8, the tool automatically chains to the imported package content. Now that we have the semantics in the model, we can create the visual model with similar colors that relate to a true UML model. Figure 7-9 shows a class diagram with a UML package view of the trees represented in Figure 7-8 using some manual package coloring and sizing.

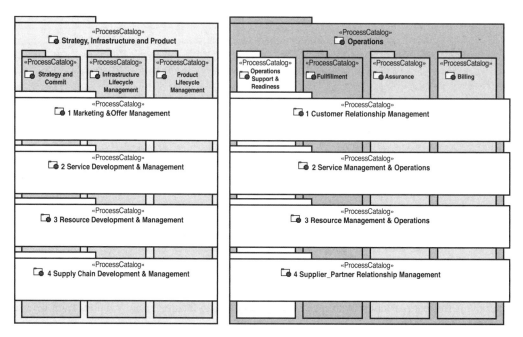

Figure 7-9   Visual two-dimensional business map using UML packages

As discussed in Chapters 1 and 5, these maps and decompositions identify boundaries for business services (see Figure 7-10). For example, the submitCustomerOrder business process is itself exposed as a service but also consumes the activateService service. This allows several implementations of the service activation with the same interface, such as activateService for DSL, activateServiceForIPTV, or activateServiceForVoIP.

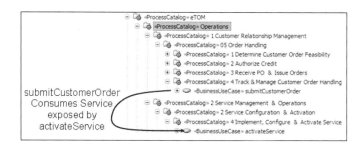

Figure 7-10   Service identification using branch boundaries

Back to the granularity discussed in Chapters 1 and 5. The use of formal business decomposition makes it obvious to locate if the business services are at a level 3 or 4 of enterprise decomposition, and as recommended, the business processes should be exposed from a level 3 and applications down to a level 4. We then look for the implementation of the service components as processes using the application and service component structures linked to the process decomposition also using a package import, as represented in Figure 7-11.

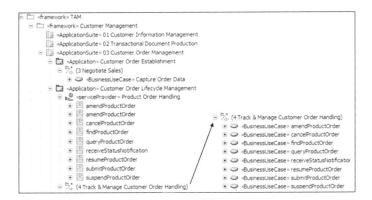

Figure 7-11   Application and Service component map decomposition captured in UML

Just as with the package import used in the business map, we can import use case packages in the application map to show which components implement what use case. This implies that there is a common package intersection of what an application implements from the business decomposition. The interfaces should be made generic to allow variations of the use cases to be exposed.

Modeling Infrastructure Layer

The last layer is the infrastructure layer that realizes the service component implementation in the applications. As shown in Figure 7-12, in Rational Software Architect for WebSphere, such topologies can be created that link the logical components with the underlying infrastructure.

Such topologies in UML are not drawings but true models with formalism. As an example, you cannot deploy an application server on the hardware without an operating system. They can be used to generate the installation and configuration scripts for topological elements in the palette, as shown in Figure 7-13.

The palette that is provided with the tool has an exhaustive model and provides support for all topology elements required in architectures. The palette has been designed to be extensible and add support for additional elements such as popular application packages. Any given configured model can be added to the palette using a right-click.

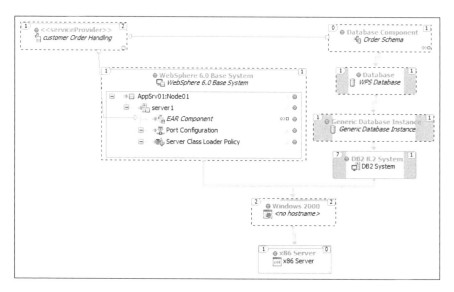

Figure 7-12   Example of customer order handling service provider in deployment topology

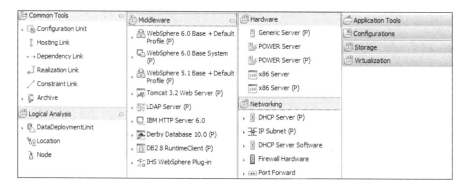

Figure 7-13   Rational Software Architect for WebSphere Topology elements palette

Modeling and Implementing Information, Services, and Processes

Using the previous maps and decompositions, we have identified the services at the right level of granularity, but we still need to specify the interfaces that include messages derived from the information model.

Information Modeling

Information modeling is classical using UML modeling. However, as information modeling sources are often provided with XML schema, the UML tools should provide the capability to import schema and convert to the equivalent UML with the appropriate stereotypes. Figure 7-14 shows a small subset of the UML model from OAGIS XML schemas imported into UML.

This XML schema has been imported using the WebSphere Business Service Fabric Toolpack add-on for Rational Software Architect.

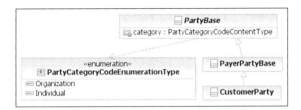

Figure 7-14   Sample from OAGIS XML schemas import in Rational

While modeling information, it is essential to structure the packages to represent the core entity domains and subdomains, as they define the boundaries for interdomain variability and namespaces. In Figure 7-15, core entity domains are as described in Chapter 3, "Implementing Dynamic Enterprise Information"—customer, enterprise, market sales, product, resource, services, and supplier partner.

Figure 7-15   Telco TMF standard SID model UML package structure

We now have to create service messages from the information models. To achieve this, we load the Software Services profile that contains the appropriate stereotypes. We then construct the message classes that aggregate the selected elements. In the message modeling, we also apply all the variability techniques described in Chapter 3, such as any type, name/values, Characteristic-Value, and so on. Figure 7-16 shows the result of the addition of a stereotype.

Figure 7-16   Stereotyped service message in UML

Next, we define the interfaces using the messages that we just modeled here.

Service Modeling

Service components have interfaces that are UML interfaces. To model a service, you just need to create a UML interface, and then add the services interface methods with the messages, as defined previously. Then we apply the service specification stereotype to the interface. This is done by selecting the Stereotypes tab and adding with the available buttons. Figure 7-17 shows the result after the stereotype has been applied.

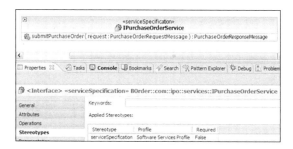

Figure 7-17   UML interface stereotyped as a service specification

We still miss a "component" that incorporates the interface and will become the service provider. For interfaces, we use a UML element to start with, which in this case is a UML component stereotyped as a serviceProvider. Then we select the component and right-click to add a UML port to the component and use the Select Existing Interface option to define the previously defined interface as the one for this component.

Then, as shown in Figure 7-18, we add the service stereotype to the port itself to complete the definition of the service component and Web Service interface.

We now have to transform the service provider components into a WSDL and the corresponding XML Schema Declaration (XSD). The UML to WSDL is the appropriate transformation in that case. UML to SOA generates SCA components with the appropriate SCDLs. Figure 7-19 shows available SOA transformations.

You have to select as a source a UML package that includes the components to transform and run the transformation appropriately. Also select the correct binding such as document/literal. After the transformation has run, you get the namespaces generated in correspondence to the UML package structure.

Business Process Modeling

In the previous sections, we mostly looked at the stable and static decompositions and how to generate the services interfaces. We now need to model and implement the dynamic part of the processes and create the flows with the appropriate process modularity.

```
⊟ 🗀 services
   ⊟ ⚲ «serviceProvider» PurchaseOrderService
      ⚙ «service» iPurchaseOrderService
   ⊟ 🔩 «serviceSpecification» IPurchaseOrderService
      ⊞ ⚙ submitPurchaseOrder ( )
```

```
                                    ⊠    «serviceProvider»
                                    ⚲   PurchaseOrderService
⚙ iPurchaseOrderService : IPurchaseOrderService
                                    ○—   🔩 IPurchaseOrderService
                                         ⚙ submitPurchaseOrder ( )
```

```
◻ Properties ⊠    ✓ Tasks  ⌨ Console  ⊞ Bookmarks  ⚲ Search  ⚲ Pattern Expl

⚲ <Component> «serviceProvider» BOrder::com::ipo::services::Pur

General         Keywords:
Attributes      Applied Stereotypes:
Operations
Stereotypes       Stereotype      Profile                 Required
                  serviceProvider | Software Services Profile  False
```

Figure 7-18   Stereotyped service provider component and port

```
⊟ 🗁 Service Oriented Architecture Transformations
      ▦ Business Process to Service Model
      ▦ Java to service model
      ▦ Session bean to service model
      ▦ UML to SOA
      ▦ UML to WSDL
      ▦ UML to XSD
      ▦ UML to XSD (deprecated)
      ▦ XSD to UML
```

Figure 7-19   Available SOA transformations

Depending on the approach you select, the round-tripping may require feedback to the initial model from elements changed in downstream tools. If you want to optimize round-tripping and avoid these feedback, you should import the services as generated from the previous modeling phase. When using WebSphere Business Modeler to model processes, you should import using the WSDL and XSD modeler import, and in the Import Option panels select the option Create Service Catalogs with File Folder Structure with the folders. Then you can ensure an exact match on export with the imported structures.

The next part is then to represent in the process modeling tool the static decompositions as a process catalog structure, as shown in Figure 7-20. This makes the crossing of functional boundaries apparent and highlights the need for the creation of separate process modules in each branch if variability is expected between these branches.

Now that we have business services and the process tree, we can start creating process modules that can be endpoints for service interfaces and then allow implementation variability by using the dynamic binding techniques described in the integration techniques.

To achieve this, you first need to create a process in the tree with the appropriate name, such as submitProductOrder, shown in Figure 7-21. But if the process implements submitProduct

Order for processing orders for individuals, it could also be named submitProductOrderProcess-ForIndividuals, and there could be other process names with the same interface for other variations. Then drop the service from the business services and wire the input and output to the input of the newly created process.

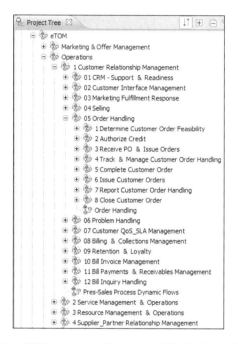

Figure 7-20   Capturing the eTOM decomposition tree in WebSphere Business Modeler

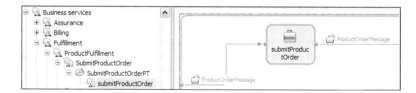

Figure 7-21   Newly created process with service dropped and wired to define interface

Then delete the service. The result is an empty process with the exact same interface definition as the service façade it implements. You can then implement the process logic as the one described in Figure 7-22.

The preceding process example is usually called by a CRM application that only knows the submitProductOrder interface. The dynamic binding resolves the endpoint as the preceding process, which first calls an application to decompose the order into telco service order, for example, DSL, IPTV, and VoIP, and then loops on as many service orders calling the same service interface with varying payloads appropriate to each telco service. The dynamic routing then resolves the different target process modules for configuring in our case DSL service, IPTV service, or VoIP service. After having documented the loop index in the process, it can generate a BPEL.

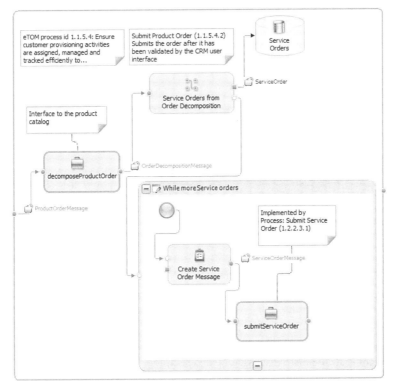

Figure 7-22   Product order process with service call in loop to call service order processes

In addition to the small process modules targeting BPEL implementation of service chore-ographies, there is a need for modeling the end-to-end process that is used in the monitoring infrastructure. We describe this in Chapter 8, "Managing and Monitoring a Dynamic BPM and SOA Environment."

These monitoring models, as shown in Figure 7-23, are high-level representations of the processes as the business management expects to track them. They define the measurement points and the information that needs to be tracked. In this monitoring model, you can use either the services messages previously imported to define the information flowing that will carry the performance indicator data or you can define new elements.

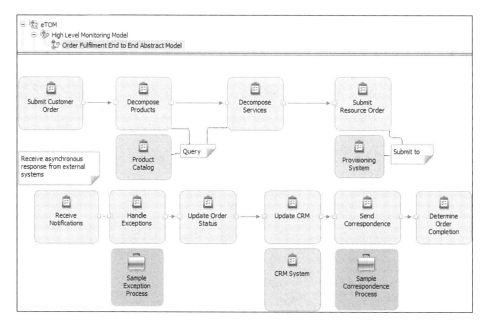

Figure 7-23   Example end-to-end model for business monitoring purposes

A monitoring model does not require the use of BPEL choreographies. You just need to instrument the infrastructure to ensure that the corresponding infrastructure messages are generated for the business monitoring.

The modeled processes are now nearly ready to be deployed either to further integration tasks, or in selected cases, to WebSphere Process Server. The necessary tasks to complement the model shown in Figure 7-23 are discussed in next section.

BPEL and Process Choreography Integration Implementation

BPMN is a notation language and not an execution language. Therefore, there is a need for converting the processes modeled as language that provides support for execution. This language is defined by the Business Process Execution Language (WS-BPEL) standard.[6]

Before detailing the tools transition from BPMN to WS-BPEL, let's examine the WS-BPEL execution language and constraints derived from the differences between these two standards. Since I am focusing on the services choreography, I do not look at other possible targets for BMPN modeling, in particular the XPDL standard, which is workflow centered and not specifically designed for services choreography.

WS-BPEL Execution Language

The Web Services Business Process Execution Language (WS-BPEL) standard targets the creation of XML documents describing specific process choreographies of Web Services. It is a model for describing simple or complex exchanges between actors exposing their activities or processes as service contracts. This language includes essential control flow and context elements to enable the execution of choreographies based on its content. The context elements define the state information elements that need to be carried forward in the process and persisted in case of long-running sequences where the responses are not immediate. In addition, the context elements are the base for correlation attributes that help return to a specific process instance in case of asynchronous interactions. If multiple instances of an ordering process are running, we need to differentiate the order of customer A from the order of customer B, particularly as the supply may take several days and in consequence the order processes will need to be persisted and restored to the corresponding order process when the appropriate provisioning tasks are completed.

The WS-BPEL business process is composed of simple or structured activities that define the behavior of the process, including loops, switches, tests, and services invocations. The resulting business process is itself a service that can be exposed as a Web Service or a Service Component Architecture (SCA) compliant component.[7]

The WS-BPEL language describes also the sequencing constraints, service flows, and identification of target services with the definition of partners providing the services. In theory, the WS-BPEL models are vendor neutral and should be portable. However, vendor differences exist, and the tools usually provide a strict compatibility mode if portability is required. Then the tools usually generate executable artifacts from the WS-BPEL documents in XML describing the processes.

The WS-BPEL language processes are structured in an overall <process> tagged XML document. This <process> contains all the necessary elements for its execution. The following list describes these elements and uses a < ... > tag name whenever a precise and unique tag defines that element:

- <partner> defines all the entities that provide or consume services.
- <variables> define the process context variables.
- Activities include all the process steps such as service invocation.
- Fault and compensation handlers manage exception in the process flow or service interactions.
- <correlationSets> define the elements identifying specific instances of processes.

The variables contain the process context, such as specific object instance data. They allow the persistence of messages shared between activities in a process and may also be used to carry any process required data, such as a loop counter. These variables are defined by XML schemas included in the consumed or exposed WSDL, but also from process specific schemas.

Variables have scope that can be global to the process, or local to a subset of activities of a process such as a compensation handler. Finally, the variables can be manipulated using an <assign> activity.

The activities define the steps of a process and correspond to statements in any programming language, such as C, Java, or Perl.

There are three types of activities in a BPEL document:

- **Service interaction activities**—Receiving a specific service request, receiving a variety of requests and selecting the appropriate one, or invoking a service request. These service interaction activities use `<receive>`, `<reply>`, and `<invoke>` tags.

- **Structured activities**—Provide sequence, flows, while loops, and switches. This category of activities uses the following tags:

  - `<sequence>` to ensure an order between activities

  - `<flow>` allows parallel process of activities

  - `<while>` to execute loops

  - `<switch>` to make decisions

  - `<pick>` to select appropriate incoming events and is a combination of receive and switch

  It is notable that there is only `<while>` for implementing loops. Similarly, although BPMN does have a branch capability, there is no such branching capability in the WS-BPEL standard. Thus it generates some BPMN to WS-BPEL translation problems described later in the chapter.

- **Utility activities**—These activities provide additional support such as defining a scope, raising exceptions, waiting, assigning values to variables, and even "do nothing."

No other functional logic is available and can be accessed through a service interaction activity.

A `<scope>` is a way to define a common context for a subset of activities included in that scope construct. Variables defined in that scope are visible only from activities inside that scope. Similarly compensation handlers or exception handlers may be defined within a specific scope only. If any of a fault handler, event handler, compensation handler, variable, or correlation set is defined with the same name of an element in a containing scope, then it supersedes that element for all activities within the scope and only for that scope. Any changes are lost when leaving the scope.

An important construct of WS-BPEL is the internal compensation model similar to a more distributed compensation model of the WS-BusinessActivity standard.[8] The principle of a compensation handler is that it identifies the "undo" actions necessary to reverse or inhibit the previously executed actions of a particular sequence or flow of activities.

Fault handlers capture any unhandled fault resulting from a service interaction such as, but not limited to, SOAP errors. They can be used to propagate errors to the caller of the process or take any other action when the error occurs. They are often used in combination with compensation handlers. The default fault handler executes all the compensation handlers in the scope of the fault and then raises the fault to the containing scope.

In the transition from modeling to choreography, it is important to note that BPMN standards and WS-BPEL standards have been developed independently and are not strictly matching.

One example that the BPMN standard allows and the current WS-BPEL standard does not is the backward connections to the input of an upstream task. However, tools such as WebSphere

Business Modeler perform the automatic correction described in Figure 7-26 to generate a valid WS-BPEL.

A backward connection (shown in Figure 7-24) is a natural way for business analysts to model that a set of activities has to be reiterated if some condition is met in later phases of a process. However, your BPMN tool may not support direct correction and translation of these constructs to WS-BPEL.

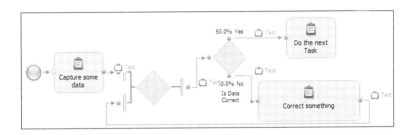

Figure 7-24   Example of backward loop in BPMN

This type of construct is not allowed in BPEL, and a slight correction of the model is required. Because the only way that BPEL has to pass data inside a while loop is through process data, the text output from the first task is preserved in local data, and a BPMN while loop is created with no input or output (see Figure 7-25).

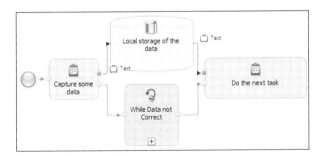

Figure 7-25   Corrected backward loop in BPMN

Inside the loop, the task gets its data from the local repository as in the equivalent BPEL. The generated BPEL then is like Figure 7-26.

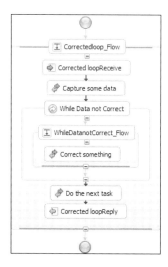

Figure 7-26   Corrected backward loop in BPEL construct

Because these transformations are performed automatically by the tools doing the export for deployment, the generated BPEL should not be changed. All changes should initiate from the process modeling tool.

From BPMN to WS-BPEL Implementation

To get this automatic support for BPMN to WS-BPEL transformation and deployment, in WebSphere Business Modeler, you can start by selecting the appropriate deployment mode. This automatically transforms constructs that can be adapted and prevents the captured constructs that are not acceptable in WS-BPEL. As Figure 7-27 shows, several other modes are available to WebSphere Business Modeler, with variable constraint levels. You may successively use several modes in the same model.

Basic	Alt+Ctrl+B
Advanced	Alt+Ctrl+A
WebSphere Business Integration Server Foundation	Alt+Ctrl+S
WebSphere MQ Workflow	Alt+Ctrl+M
✔ WebSphere Process Server	Alt+Ctrl+P
FileNet Business Process Manager	Alt+Ctrl+F
WebSphere Business Services Fabric	Alt+Ctrl+W

Figure 7-27   WebSphere Process Server mode in WebSphere Integration Developer

This WebSphere Process Server mode allows process modeling for constructs that can be deployed in BPEL. To be deployable, the process model needs to be complete and all activities configured. To detail the complementary tasks, I use the process in Figure 7-28, which is a real example of a process in Modeler that blocks and unblocks an IP phone line resource, in case some problem occurs with that Voice over IP (VoIP) account.

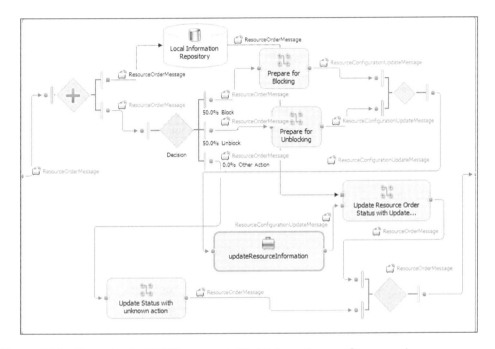

Figure 7-28   Example of a BMPN process in WebSphere Process Server mode

To eliminate all errors in the process model shown in Figure 7-28, for a valid direct deployment, we need to specify all maps, process data, loops, and decision points with appropriate data elements. In the process in Figure 7-28, we need to define the Update Resource Order Status and Update Resource result data maps and particularly how they copy header data and payload data from the previous service interactions (from TeleManagement Forum's Multi-Technology Operations System Interface [TMF MTOSI] standard) to the original ResourceOrderMessage that will be passed back to process caller. This data map can be entered visually, and the user interface is shown in Figure 7-29.

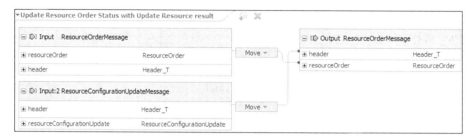

Figure 7-29   Mapping objects in WebSphere Business Modeler

Then the process can be exported to WebSphere Integration Developer, as shown in Figure 7-30, where service components can be aggregated and integrated if necessary or directly deployed to WebSphere Process Server.

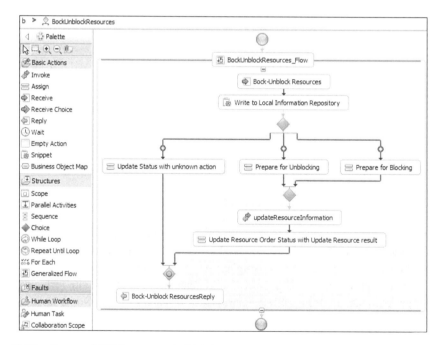

Figure 7-30   Exported BPEL process in WebSphere Integration Developer

To avoid round-tripping problems and allow direct deployment, the process should always be modified from the modeler environments. The specific elements that you may want to address in the service integration development are service component wiring. Figure 7-31 shows the wiring diagram for the assembly of the process with inbound requesters or outbound services, which in this case could be provided by adapters to existing applications as shown in the palette.

The export process from WebSphere Business Modeler also generates the template mediations that would be required to access a specific consumed service such as one of the outbound adapters shown in the palette of Figure 7-31. The template mediation is located in the generated implementation project and is directly executable as shown in Figure 7-32.

Figure 7-31   Process SCA component wiring

Figure 7-32   Template mediation code generated by the export

After the mediation coding, when the wiring is completed and unit tests achieved, you can deploy the processes to the target systems. The deployment topology that we reviewed in the preceding sections can make reference to the specific Enterprise ARchives (EARs) containing the processes and have topology scripting integrated into the deployment in a more enterprise IT management controlled approach.

Testing Processes and Services

Testing a module you created in the component assembly diagram editor is easy. You just need to right-click and select Test Module. You then get access to the test client where you can specify which event and interface to test, and you also can input specific data for your test. An example of this process is shown in Figure 7-33.

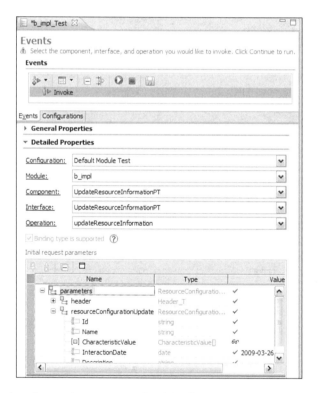

Figure 7-33   Interface for service component unit testing

You can store any unit test result and then reuse these in test suites you also create in the same tool. However, there may be a need for running more complex test cases including scripting with variability of the input and output, over predefined test suites. This is the purpose of IBM Rational Service Tester for SOA Quality V8.0 that enables the creation and execution of automated functional tests of services without a user interface.

A particular focus is required when testing processes that include human interactions with GUIs and with task escalations timers set to several days. In that particular case, you either need to use the process engine API to interact with the tasks programmatically to act on behalf of the user or for the escalation duration tests you may in addition need to change the timers to a viable time for the test cycle, or in some cases attempt to change the system clocks to accelerate the time. In the latter case, you must be careful not to affect the overall behavior of your systems and ensure that you do that in isolation.

Summary

In this chapter, we looked at the enterprise architecture chain from requirements to the various architectural layers, implementation of processes, and integration of components. Other dynamicity and variability methods elements were described in previous chapters looking at variable information with ontologies and other constructs, processes, and integration layers with the dynamic binding policies. The runtime aspects and the associated tooling are explored in Chapter 8.

CHAPTER **8**

Managing and Monitoring a Dynamic BPM and SOA Environment

Anticipate the difficult by managing the easy.

Lǎozǐ

Managing and Monitoring Flexible Processes and SOA

Implementing dynamic BPM and SOA does not relieve the enterprise from employing a holistic management and monitoring approach on the business and IT levels. In previous chapters, we looked at using variability techniques to add damping in the causal chain, which removes the strong correlation between consumer and provider. This damping may be seen as an inhibitor to an end-to-end management and monitoring process; however, it is still necessary to manage the business services facing the customer as a complete stack to anticipate and correct problems that arise. Borrowing a line from a well-known rhyme, "for the want of a nail... the battle was lost," let's look at some of the nails, horses, and riders that help win the SOA and BPM battle.

The SOA and BPM management space is broad and has several dimensions. Figure 8-1 shows the relationships between these dimensions and/or elements.

In this chapter, we do not address the full SOA governance, which is well covered in existing literature, but we look specifically at the life cycle and management aspects. SOA management includes planning and organizing, program management control, development of processes and services as well as the operations of processes and services across these management domains.

- **Business processes and services life cycle**—The policies, rules, and processes that define how the BPM and SOA environment functions consistently across the enterprise.

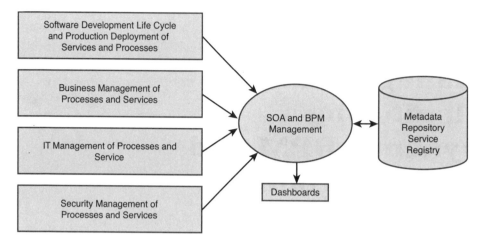

Figure 8-1   SOA and BPM management elements

- **Business management of processes and business services**—The mechanism for defining, implementing, and delivering the status of business operations as well as providing accurate, real-time information about the state of the business delivering this management information with the appropriate aggregated Key Performance Indicators (KPIs).

- **IT processes and service management**—A consolidated set of practices and operations that are applied to all levels of IT management (process, service, application, and technology infrastructure) that provide a mechanism for the execution of management and control policies of the technology layers.

  For the SOA and BPM space, management and control policies specifically include

  - Process choreography and services component management, or the application of IT services management processes specifically for the process automation control as well as service component management, including design, development, and runtime infrastructure.

  - Management of the applications that provide the services business logic.

  - Management of the middleware and hardware technology infrastructure that serves as the base to operate the application, services, and business processes.

  - Cross layer business service management, or analyzing the impact of lower layers on the delivered services and processes. This management attempts to answer the questions which and how many business services and processes are affected if a particular device or middleware instance fails. Am I able to deliver the expected quality of service?

- **Security**—Addresses the design and deployment of a common security model and consolidated security mechanisms across all aspects of the processes, software services application, and technology environment. I'm addressing security separately because it is so pervasive; it impacts all the other domains and requires specific attention.

All these domains use a metadata repository to provide a "logical" focal point for all metadata that relates to the design, build, and run phases of a BPM and SOA deployment. Even though this repository appears as a single point, it can federate other specific domain repositories and enables a global consolidation of the various policies. Having a logical focal point provides a place to perform impact analysis when changes occur in any of the layers. The registry should provide support for questions such as

- Which services and processes are affected by a change in the data sharing model used for integration?
- Which processes are affected by a service operation interface change?

Business Processes and Services Life Cycle Management

The three main artifact domains involved in a business process and business services dynamic approach require specific life cycle management. These domains, as described in Chapter 3, "Implementing Dynamic Enterprise Information," Chapter 4, "Implementing Variable Services," and Chapter 5, "Implementing Dynamic Business Processes," are the service information model and policies, the business services operations, and the business processes.

Service Information Model Life Cycle Management

This domain includes the management of changes in the information model and consists of four steps:

1. Import and integrate model changes.
2. Model comparison.
3. Impact analysis.
4. Change action selection.

Import and Integrate Models

The changes in the information definition can come to the IT in various formats: XML schemas, UML models, or database Data Definition Language (DDL) files. A common service information model must be defined. As explained in Chapter 3, this model should describe the semantics of the information and messages exposed by services; it can be UML with appropriate stereotypes, XML schemas, or any other standardized representation, but a unique metadata format should serve as a reference for the information model.

For example, the TeleManagement Forum defines three standards that include information models: the SID model in UML, the MTOSI standard for XML schemas in XSD, and Operations Support System for Java (OSS/J) interfaces and classes. If all three sources are used, it would be appropriate to select XML, XSD, or Java for the data format presentation, although UML is probably the most versatile in this case because it allows the modeling of both Java and XML and consolidation of all models in UML. UML platforms usually provide XSD or Java import features.

Since we want to consolidate the diverse sources and model formats that constitute an enterprise model, we need the appropriate transformation capabilities. Rational Software Architect (RSA) provides support for developing any custom transformation between models. One enterprise may tune these transformations to standardize and automate the initial model load and transformation to the common metadata representation.

Figure 8-2 is an example of the consolidation of XML schemas to UML, using import in RSA. This import of an XSD in a UML model uses a plug-in provided by the WebSphere Fabric Tool Pack.

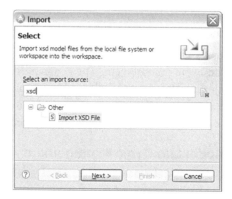

Figure 8-2   XML schema import RSA add-on in the WebSphere Fabric Tool Pack[1]

An XML format of the models has to be produced from the common model because the service registries available on the market usually only support XML schemas to represent information models.[2]

At each iteration change of the information model, possibly resulting from new releases of standards, new business information needed, and any information source change, a new consolidated model will be versioned. Once the models have been loaded and consolidated for that version, we can move on to the model comparison step to identify changes from a previous version of the model if one existed.

Model Comparison

The model comparison highlights the differences between the new version of an information model and a previous version of the model. In our case, we are mostly looking at version differences between the consolidated models. As shown in Figure 8-3, any additions, changes, or deletions are examined.

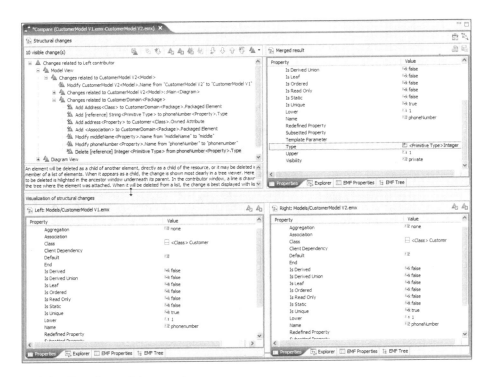

Figure 8-3 Sample model comparison

Once the model comparison is reviewed and information changes are accepted or the new version of the consolidated model adjusted, we can move on to the model adjustment process. In this process, we apply all the variability techniques described in Chapter 3 to avoid propagating to interface changes that could be absorbed by information variability. We're interested in propagating only fundamental structural changes of the information model used for integrations and services.

Impact Analysis

The goal of an impact analysis is to determine the global effect of a change to a particular artifact, in our case, starting from the information model. An impact analysis identifies the specific artifact to be modified, and then traces back through any relationships that indicate a dependency on that artifact. Normally with a variability approach, the impact analysis should show a limited number of WSDL, BPELs, or other components.

This process generates a complete graph, starting at the selected artifact and finishing with artifacts on which nothing else depends. Each artifact in the graph could therefore be affected by the change to the selected artifact. The artifact content types that can be affected by information model changes include XML schemas, Web Service descriptions, and any mapping mediation that uses the schema.

Figure 8-4 is a specific plug-in that my team developed to perform such analysis in RSA and identify the specific elements of a Web Services model that are impacted by an information change.

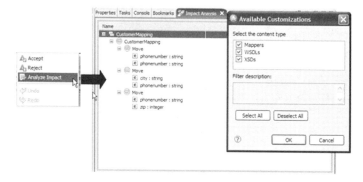

Figure 8-4   Example of a RSA plug-in developed to perform impact analysis

Figure 8-5 is an example of the impact analysis available out of the box from WebSphere Registry and Repository.

Name	Description	Object Type	Version	Impact Relationship	Relationship Name	Originating Object
TrueOrFalseBO.xsd	Boolean BO	XML schema definition		Depends on	includedSchemas	http.tonawanda.sr.ibm.com.base.xsd
CustomerBO.xsd	Customer BO	XML schema definition		Depends on	includedSchemas	http.tonawanda.sr.ibm.com.base.xsd
AddressBO.xsd	Address BO	XML schema definition		Depends on	includedSchemas	CustomerBO.xsd
AddressBO.xsd	Address BO	XML schema definition		Depends on	importedSchemas	CustomerBO.xsd
ContactBO.xsd	Contact BO	XML schema definition		Depends on	includedSchemas	http.tonawanda.sr.ibm.com.base.xsd
AddressBO.xsd	Address BO	XML schema definition		Depends on	includedSchemas	http.tonawanda.sr.ibm.com.base.xsd
TrueOrFalseBO.xsd	Boolean BO	XML schema definition		Depends on	importedSchemas	http.tonawanda.sr.ibm.com.base.xsd
CustomerBO.xsd	Customer BO	XML schema definition		Depends on	importedSchemas	http.tonawanda.sr.ibm.com.base.xsd
ContactBO.xsd	Contact BO	XML schema definition		Depends on	importedSchemas	http.tonawanda.sr.ibm.com.base.xsd
AddressBO.xsd	Address BO	XML schema definition		Depends on	importedSchemas	http.tonawanda.sr.ibm.com.base.xsd

Impact analysis results

XSD Documents > http.tonawanda.sr.ibm.com.base.xsd > Impact analysis results

This is the collection of entities that may be impacted by changes to the entity XML schema definition document http.tonawanda.sr.ibm.com.base.xsd.

Total: 10

Figure 8-5   WebSphere Registry and Repository impact analysis

In the registry, this impact analysis usually results in notifications to stakeholders. After all actors in the governance model have decided on either accepting or rejecting the impact of the information model changes, different actions can be taken depending on how the change is to be deployed.

Change Action Selection

If we accept the changes, this step may imply changing and testing many interfaces and processes.

In a dynamic approach, we want to limit the impact of a change from the provider side on consumers of services, and vice versa. So, the change action can be to provide an adaptation for the existing consumers from the model they are using to the model as it evolves. The automatic generation of mapping mediations or mapping services is one that can be particularly useful in making the impact of changes smoother and providing variability.

The examples in Figure 8-6 show a business object data transformation generated from the impact analysis step.

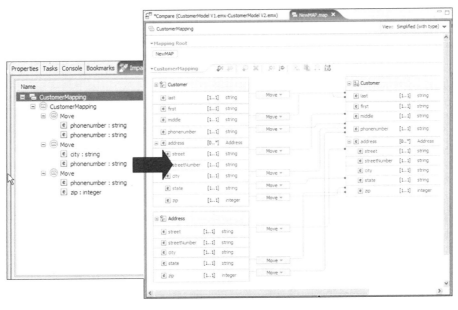

Figure 8-6   Business object mapping generation from an impact analysis

Instead of a data mapping in mediation, the wrappering in a service of the adaptation of different information model object mapping provides additional reusability.

A service that does this adaptation is as follows:

```
newInformationModel serviceVersionMap(oldInformationModel)
```

Business Service Life Cycle Management

Flexibility is the goal of the approach discussed throughout this book, allowing the services interfaces flexible limits to accommodate the need for change. Still, we have to manage the services life cycle with the appropriate versioning approach. Neither the Web Services nor Service Component Architecture standards, discussed in Chapter 4, define anything specific to service versioning. The granularity of the descriptors defined by these two standards is at the service component level not at the operation level.

The identification elements for services provided by these two standards are name and namespace. The implication here is that a version strategy that relies solely on public domain elements can only be based on name and namespace combinations. The namespace content ends up being the natural carrier for public version information because the composition of service names is usually purely linked to the semantic of the business service.

Including major version numbers in the namespace is common. For example, Web Services Reliable Messaging defines these rules.[3] Listing 8-1 speaks to best practices for versioning.

Listing 8-1   Defining Best Practices for Versioning

Namespace URI Versioning Policy
The pattern of the WS-Reliable Messaging **v1.1** namespace URI shall be:
    http://docs.oasis-open.org/ws-rx/wsrm/yyyymm
Where yyyymm is the century, year and month chosen by the TC for that
version of the namespace URI.

Other common approaches put major versions in the namespace and reserve minor versions for the nonbackward compatible services definition, such as deletion of elements in the information model or of operations. Modifications that do not generate backward compatibility issues, do not impact the namespaces.

The Web Services Business Activity standard states:

"Under this policy, these are examples of backwards compatible changes that would not result in assignment of a new namespace URI:
* Addition of new global element, attribute, complexType and simpleType definitions.
* Addition of new operations within a WSDL portType or binding (along with the corresponding schema, message and part definitions).
* Addition of new elements or attributes in locations covered by a previously specified wildcard.
* Modifications to the pattern facet of a type definition for which the value-space of the previous definition remains valid or for which the value-space of the preponderance of instance would remain valid.
* Modifications to the cardinality of elements for which the value-space of possible instance documents conformant to the previous revision of the schema would still be valid with regards to the revised cardinality rule."[4]

An alternate solution resolves services endpoints using a services registry.[5] Then the registry description can include a version attribute in addition to the name and the namespace. With a services registry, the version attribute can be defined at the operation level. This operation level of version control, however, implies an additional management effort, and it should be carefully evaluated based on requirements and the benefits to the cost of service operation changes.

Open SOA aligned registries include APIs to select SCA, WSDL, XML schemas, or any other document. Listing 8-2 is an example of code to retrieve a specific Web Service description from the registry.

Listing 8-2   Example Code to Retrieve Web Service Description from Registry

```
// Example code to retrieve myService.wsdl with a version string of "2.0"
PropertyQuery propertyQuery = (PropertyQuery)
DataFactory.INSTANCE.create(TypeConstants.SR_URI,
TypeConstants.TYPE_PROPERTYQUERY);
        String xpath = "/WSRR/WSDLDocument[@name='myService" " +
"and @version='2.0' and @namespace='http://com.ibm.wsrr.samples/wsdl']";
propertyQuery.setQueryExpression(xpath);
```

Enterprise Services Buses now provide registry endpoint lookup mediations that simplify such queries. Figure 8-7 is an example of mediation as provided by the WebSphere Enterprise Service Bus.

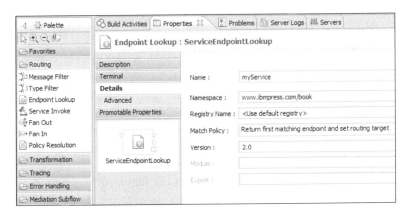

Figure 8-7   Endpoint lookup mediation configuration

The policy determines the number of endpoints that will be added to the message if one or more matches are retrieved. These are the possible scenarios:

- **Return all matching endpoints**—Updates the message with the service information of all the retrieved endpoints. You then need to use another mediation primitive to select a service.

- **Return first matching endpoint and set routing target**—Retrieves the service information of one of the matched endpoints, based on the values of the classification and user properties. The message is routed to the retrieved endpoint, if the Use Dynamic check box is enabled on the callout node or service invoke primitive.

- **Return all matching endpoints and set alternate routing targets**—Sets the target as the first retrieved endpoint and uses the remaining matches to set the alternate targets.

You can use the Return All Matching Endpoints policy to choose a specific service in the mediation flow. Then, select the service by using another mediation primitive.

Business Process Life Cycle Management

The evolving business conditions require an enterprise to adapt its operating modes resulting in the enterprise's business abstract processes constantly evolving. In Chapter 5, you saw how the modularization can reduce the impact of changes, but there will still be instances of a business process that may last a considerable duration (in some cases, months or even years), and changes made to the definition of a business process might be required to be applied to already existing process instances as well as to instances newly created against that definition. We had such cases of existing processes that needed to be changed on-the-fly, in governmental projects where the law changed and had to be applied to existing instance processes so that the next steps would follow the new law.

Such business processes have a set of steps that execute on the runtime environment when they are active and a set of intermediate stages when they are awaiting an external stimulus, such as a human user processing a manual step. As described in previous chapters, these processes are composed of chains of private processes that collectively have an implicit state that requires synchronization in case of evolution. The likelihood of a change to the process definition impacting existing long-running abstract or private process (as defined in Chapter 1) instances depends on the duration of such instances and is relative to the particular domain.

Process definitions are generally formalized using flows, such as described by BPMN, choreographies (BPEL), state machines (UML), or ad-hoc sequencing models. Generally, these formalisms deal with two basic concepts: nodes, which can be services, activities, or actions; and flow of control, which are the connectors between nodes. In any running process instance, an implied state is associated with where that particular instance is within the overall process definition. Any changes in the specification of the nature of the nodes or in the semantics of the flow of control expressed by connections between nodes imply a process definition change, which we want to limit as much as possible in a variability approach. By experience, the system test on a process definition change can take a long validation cycle and imply a high cost, which is why we want to limit changes.

The following patterns are meant for handling changes in the process definition, which go beyond changes that can be immediately applied to existing process instances:

- **Abstract processes dynamic binding approach**—This approach, described in Chapter 4, is sometimes referred to as **implicit process definition**. Multiple services (or processes) are interconnected via dynamic binding resolved at runtime using contract-, content-, or context-based policies. The overall abstract process definition can be changed by either changing the policies or replacing, changing, or adding any of the chained process definitions. This is the approach that allows the most dynamicity.

- **Module decomposition with a late binding approach**—This approach is used in the case of a single private process definition coordinating lower level subprocesses. Each subprocess is called using a late binding approach, meaning that the definition used is the subprocess definition in use at the time the parent process makes the subprocess calls with the appropriate service interface. The subprocess definition can change without having to change the top-level process in case the input and output parameters to this subprocess are not affected. This approach offers less dynamicity for the overall process flow than the first modular approach.

- **Blind replay navigation approach**—We can model a BPEL process definition so that a process instance of a new version can navigate "blindly" from one activity to another without actually executing anything based on some external properties that resolve preexisting instance completion state. This allows for effectively skipping over the activities the instance running against the old definition had already completed. Once the process instance has been navigated to reach the desired state, it can then continue executing the respective steps against the changed definition. This approach is a tactical approach used in migrations of existing processes. However, it implies that the processes versions are close enough to perform a blind replay approach.

- **Refactoring: Changing the name of the process definition**—If there is a requirement to run multiple concurrent versions of a process definition to be available at runtime the only way to achieve this is by literally creating a new process definition (versus a new version) by copying the old process definition and applying a new name. This approach is only valid from a business aspect to let the current process instances complete with their current logic.

One way to implement the blind replay listed previously is to use process engine APIs to programmatically interact with the process instances. You should note that the WS-BPEL standard does not yet formalize a way of externalizing state of processes in terms of what current activities are being performed. However, specific implementation does provide APIs, such as IBM Web-Sphere Process Server (WPS) "com.ibm.bpe.api" interfaces, to manage and query processes. This process server engine exposes getAllWorkItems()[6] and claimAndComplete() interfaces that can be used to retrieve the pending work items for a particular process instance and make them progress.

The Workflow Management Coalition standards body in its interface 2 document does standardize the API WMOpenActivityInstancesList that enables querying all completed activities within a specific workflow that then use WMGetWorkItem and WMCompleteWorkItem to handle the items' progress.

Operational Management

Operational management domain addresses the support elements that maintain performance and availability of business processes, services, applications, and supporting IT infrastructure. It looks at protecting and maximizing the usage and availability of these assets.

It provides the support to visualize the health of business processes and services and service level agreements. Using these tools the IT management team can then isolate, diagnose, and fix the highest-priority transaction performance problems, and target IT resources and actions to quickly resolve the most critical and costly issues to deliver the greatest impact to the business.

As shown in Figure 8-8, operational management looks at managing the following layers:

- Technology infrastructure including hardware, operating systems, and middleware.

- Applications and application components, either Common Off The Shelf (COTS) applications, such as SAP, Siebel, and Oracle, or J2EE or .Net applications.

- Services and services components that are the services oriented enablement of applications and application components.

- Business process instances, specifically the operational status of choreographies of private processes. The business monitoring is addressed in the next section.

Information is pervasive and managed as required on each layer.

The operational management also looks at correlating the layers into a dependency tree that help anticipating problems on higher layers that would derive from problems occurring in the supporting layers. Of course, the end user also has management as the consumer of the stack, shown in Figure 8-8.

Operational management requires the deployment of appropriate agents for specific management purposes and usually looks at reusing all existing logs and management interfaces, such as application or infrastructure events logs, but also Simple Network Management Protocol (SNMP) events or Java Management Extensions (JMX) interfaces.

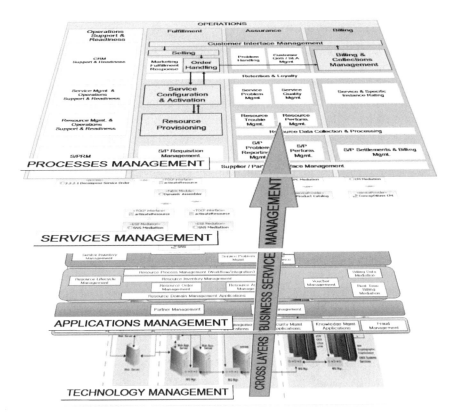

Figure 8-8 Operational management layers

Technology Management Layer

This management layer manages resources, supporting middleware, and transaction performance.

Resource management consists of collecting and analyzing resource data such as CPU utilization, network latency, I/O throughput, operating system status. The typical problems that can be detected at this level are network or hardware device queues filling up or timing out, disk failures, and hardware or network failures.

The supporting middleware management consists of understanding the health of the application servers, transactional servers, and database and integration infrastructure that support the services and then correlating problems in the services to infrastructure issues such as a messaging middleware queue filling up or a an exhausted thread pool.

Application Management Layer

This management layer manages application components and provides contextual resource monitoring across application resources. It looks at providing a consistent view of performance and availability metrics across multiple application resources. Applications can have memory leaks, performance issues, traps, or exceptions. Examples of application monitoring are mySAP memory and performance monitoring reported by mySAP service; Siebel eBusiness resources, databases, transactions, users, applications, subapplications, or programs; and application server component data coming from EJBs, servlets, JCAs, and JDBCs. It also provides support across the monitoring layers to establish the relationship between service requests and the application implementation artifacts such as COTS applications, but also J2EE beans and JDBC requests.

Service Management Layer

This management layer address services management, which looks first at collecting services data such as service headers, payload (SOAP/XML), caller origin, service destination, and service characteristics. It specifically looks at detecting SLA violations, invalid services requests, and dependency or relationship mismatch. It highlights Web Service response times, particularly the ones that exceed thresholds and some messages that are exceptionally long. Figure 8-9 is an example screen capture of the service management tool that shows the response time of services calls.

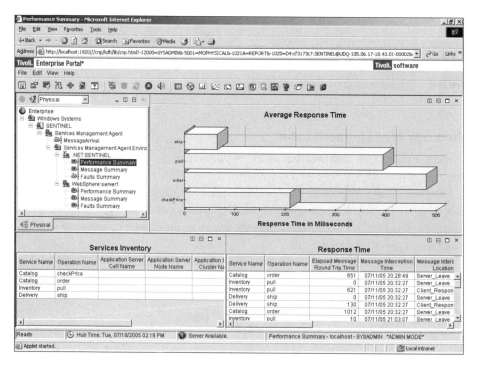

Figure 8-9   Service management in IBM Tivoli® Composite Application Management for SOA

It should track to meet service level commitments by alerting problems before these levels are violated and have support for quickly isolating problems to minimize outages.

Through the use of correlation elements in the service message payloads, it can control the message flow in the service environment. In addition, the tooling and monitoring provides understanding of the performance of a service as decomposition information transactions composed of individual requests.

Figure 8-10 is an example of control flow management using such agents that show dependency and sequence diagrams built from the agent correlation information.

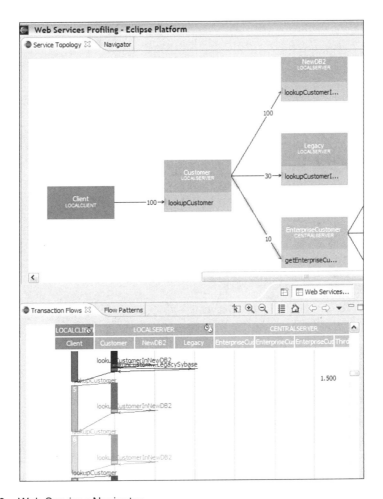

Figure 8-10   Web Services Navigator

As shown in Figure 8-11, the management infrastructure also supports the understanding of how services relate to each other and to the IT infrastructure.

Maintaining these dependencies is essential to anticipating service problems that arise from application, middleware, or hardware problems.

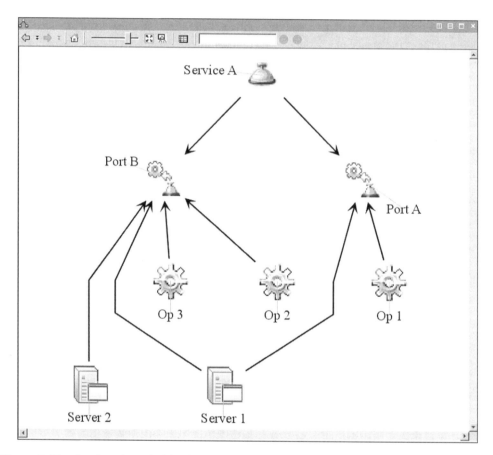

Figure 8-11   Services to underlying layers dependency tree

Business Processes Operational Management

The business process management focuses on business process flow health, detecting and alerting on anomalous conditions that could affect the business processes. It also provides the correlation between individual service health and the health of processes that are using such services.

This management involves two aspects: the ability to list and act on running processes and the management of impact of underlying operational layer status. The first type of management interface is provided out of the box by the process engines, which have API and default visualization management interfaces not requiring any additional management software, such as the Choreography Explorer (see Figure 8-12) shipped with WebSphere Process Server.

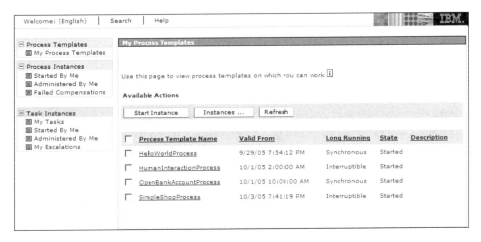

Figure 8-12   Default Choreography Explorer interface

In addition to this process instance view a dependency view can be provided linking processes, services, and the infrastructure. Figure 8-13 is the process detailed view from Tivoli ITCAM for SOA that helps manage all the SOA artifacts that a business process requires.[7]

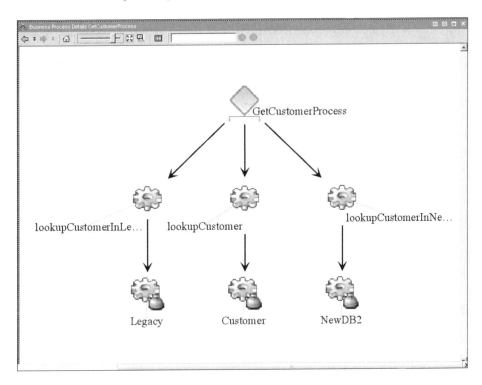

Figure 8-13   Process detailed dependency management view

Dynamic Business Process Management

There are two aspects to management of business processes: The first part is specific business process instances tracking, and the second part is global business monitoring with reports or scorecards on KPIs. Both aspects require that events be collected to allow the real-time monitoring and management at the appropriate business decomposition levels. It is then important to include the design of the event capture in the technology architecture and to evaluate the message volume impact that these events generate. Our experience shows that, in many cases, the event capture strategy is not selective enough and causes performance problems, because the appropriate decomposition level approach has not been performed to select essential events.

Managing Business Monitoring Levels

This is a different monitoring process, separate from the operational monitoring discussed previously, because here we are looking not only at the choreographed processes (private processes). We are also examining the end-to-end process realized from the cascade of explicit processes in process engines and implicit processes delivered by the business logic running in packaged applications or legacy applications.

As described in previous chapters, in a dynamic business process approach the chain of private process modules realizing the end-to-end business process may result from a dynamic composition. The monitoring models that represent the explicit or implicit processes at various decomposition levels are a key part of monitoring. Following the same decomposition principles described in Chapter 1 and in Chapter 5, we use a hierarchical monitoring approach, with different monitoring levels showing different levels of processes.

Figure 8-14 shows a simplified example of an order provisioning, where the entry starts in a portal. When the customer decides to buy a product, the process switches to a CRM package. Then the order is decomposed into services for which configuration and provisioning are controlled by a set of BPEL choreographies using services that expose the telco service configuration and activation delivered by packaged applications and the resource provisioning business logic running in legacy applications.

The business management usually requires the monitoring of the high-level view of the end-to-end process, which is realized in different systems and applications in Figure 8-14 and represented by the events numbered 1 to 7. In a dynamic approach, there is no overarching process but a chain of applications and process components lined by business services. This implies that the monitoring applications can define and incorporate monitoring models that are not the representation of a concrete choreography in one given engine, but an implicit representation of the sequence of the appropriate level of end-to-end process by providing essential events happening in the different applications.

Each application or BPEL linked in the end-to-end chain has its own low-level monitoring. It is important not to mix these low levels in the high level end-to-end monitoring, but rather allow the drill down from the high level to lower levels. This dynamic linking of monitoring levels allows the lower levels to have variations that do not impact the higher levels and thus limits the impact of changes in specific lower levels of processing.

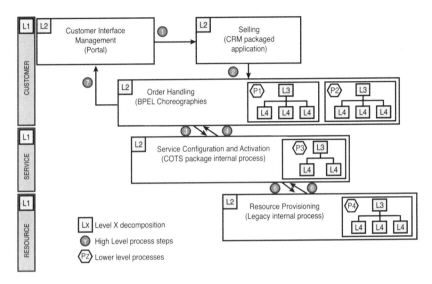

Figure 8-14   Typical end-to-end process decomposition

Variations from lower levels can still be shown in higher level process monitoring by using colors or specific labeling as shown in Figure 8-15, where variations monitored are the provision URI context for PC (in red) or for Mobile phone (in green) and the billing system variations per location.

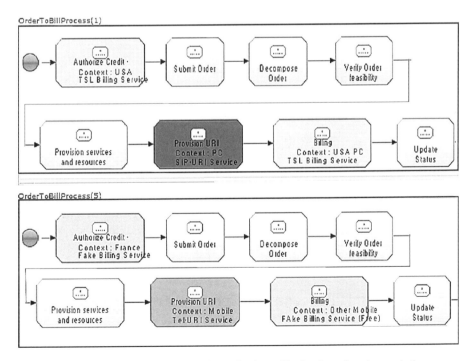

Figure 8-15   Two instances of end-to-end monitoring with shading showing variations

By selecting actions on the specific boxes, a linkage may be provided to the specific lower level monitoring, which can be application specific and provided by the specific application software vendor.

By using this decomposition approach, fewer events get to be propagated at the enterprise level and performance maintained, while deeper levels of monitoring are still available by relying on specific domain features.

Implementing Business Dashboards

Because a manageable monitoring event strategy requires fewer capture points, the KPIs should also be structured so that a single event can carry a tree of indicator measures. It should be noted that the same KPI may appear at different business domain decomposition levels.

In Figure 8-16, we see insurance policies and claims. The Financial and Operating KPIs are aggregated at the enterprise level but also at the specific domain level, such as premiums revenue evaluation. The events carrying the information must then carry enough categorization to enable the monitoring dashboards to locate the appropriate information and build the corresponding measures.

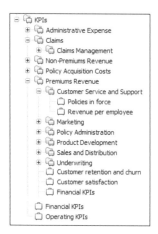

Figure 8-16   Sample structure of insurance policies and claim KPIs

Such monitoring event structures may become variable and complex. This is why the monitoring engines support user-defined functions to perform such analysis and create the appropriate measures for the dashboards. WebSphere Business Monitor provides user-defined XPath functions (UDXF), which extend the basic monitoring capability to any required type of metrics support.[8]

Securing a Dynamic Process and Services Environment

Managing security is a topic that can fill an entire book by itself. This book takes a complementary approach to the existing literature, so this section only addresses some of the high-level elements to provide initial guidance and recommendation concerning the security of a flexible processes and services environment. This section addresses only the specific elements that concern services and processes and not behavioral security, which is a more general IT security management approach.

Overall Context of Services Security

As always, in a security approach, the protection responses must be in relation to the expected threats. The new threat exposures that a services and business process approach introduce are the unauthorized used of services, including denial of service, or inappropriate use of processes or services, such as bypassing audit controls, process control validations, or authorization levels. It is particularly important to understand that services often link the user to the application logic and that a significant level of security handling must occur at that level. Using a representation similar to the Open Systems Interconnection (OSI) seven-layer model, we can represent the various security interactions that occur. As it can be seen in Figure 8-17, Web Services security occurs at layer 6, even though an HTTP authentication may require additional security to authorize the specific service operation. In addition, specific encryption and signatures may be required to prevent unauthorized eyes from looking at the services payload and to validate that the service interaction content has not been tampered with before reaching the target application providing the service. Figure 8-17 shows a layered service security model for reference.

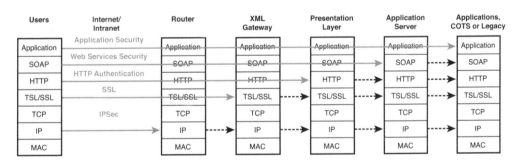

Figure 8-17 OSI-like layered service security model

Looking at the left part of in Figure 8-17, when enterprises expose services publicly, they are open ports on the Internet. These become potential entry points for hackers that try to use those services. Thus these newly opened entries need to be protected, and now XML gateways include XML security level validation that chokes undesired payloads before they reach application servers. Given the potential amount of requests, such as between enterprises interacting with partners providing content or services, these gateways are now often appliances dedicated to such functions. IBM provides the DataPower appliances that specifically perform such SOAP and XML level filtering, authentication, and validation.[9]

Another implication of sharing services with partners is that one enterprise cannot expect to manage the direct identification and authentication of all potential consumers of a service. This is why federated identity models have been developed for the use of services. These models promote the use of trustees on each partner side, providing certification of the service consumer. Several standards are being used in the field, specifically WS-Federation[10] and Liberty Alliance Federation Framework (ID-FF)[11] with a consolidation of all federated security models in Security Assertion Markup Language (SAML) 2.0 standard.[12] The federation protocols also provide support for internal single sign-on in the enterprise and managing the appropriate tokens.

The team managing the security then also has to manage the life cycle of users or trustees and of all related security tokens and certificates. This life cycle includes the initial workflow for verification and validation of credentials that occurs for any new authorized user. The impact of this workflow should not be underestimated as it requires multiple eyes in the enterprise for high value services and thus generates delays and cost.

A reasonable approach to lower security management cost is to precisely evaluate threats and risks and revert to lower layer security features, such as SSL or IPsec where sufficient. This evaluation is part of the security governance of the enterprise that defines the security policies and the compliances to these policies.

For further details, I recommend reading the free downloadable IBM Redbook® "Understanding SOA Security Design and Implementation," which gives a detailed technical description of the security.[13]

Overall Context of Processes Security

Interestingly, none of the standards looking at business process modeling, management, workflow, or choreography addresses process security. The specific choreography engine implementations, however, do look at integrating security. In end-to-end process chains, as discussed previously, the process engines or applications often interact with multiple actors, and these components by default run using middleware level credentials such as the database connection pools that open with credentials that have nothing to do with the future users of the connection.

So the security questions that process designers have to answer include

- Is the initiator of any process entitled to do so and how can I control that entitlement?

- Given who initiated the process or any of the involved actors, are the next actors entitled to interact with the process?

- Is there a need deriving from a legal policy or enterprise policy to capture an audit trail of all the actors that have been interacting in a given process module or end-to-end abstract process?

Propagating the Credentials of the Initiator of a BPEL Process

If the inbound protocol that instantiates the BPEL process supports security credentials, WS-*, or Java enterprise credentials, then they are propagated by the most popular BPEL engines.[14]

If the protocol carrying the process instantiation request cannot carry the security information such as pure JMS (as opposed to SOA or JMS), then of course, the BPEL engine will run
under its static security credential definitions.

Propagating the Credentials of the Initiator of an End-to-End Heterogeneous Process

In that case, all the applications and process engines linked in the chain of the process and business logic must be able to carry the credentials to the next module.

If one application in the chain cannot carry the security credentials, then a mediation in the
Enterprise Service Bus can be used to correlate requests and reinsert credentials, but this may end
up being complex and is used only in the specific cases that require such a security level.

Ensuring that the Involved Actors Are Entitled to Interact with the Process

In an enterprise security approach, all human actors are authenticated, so the process implementers must ensure that the process engines are able to define roles, groups, or users that can act
on specific human tasks required by the processes. The commonly used security granularity at the
process level is group level, usually getting that information from a Lightweight Directory Access
Protocol (LDAP)–based directory infrastructure.

Managing an Audit Trail

It is a common practice for engines that involve human interaction to provide an audit trail.[15] However, if the process is a combination of packaged or proprietary applications, process flows, and
legacy applications, there will be a need for defining additional audit capture points and a global
audit management strategy to integrate the various audit trails into a consolidated one. Volumes
can become important; for example, the financial transactions retention requirements can span several years and lead to terabytes of audit trail.

Payload Level Services Security Performance Implications

The security architecture must take into account the impact on performance of message level
encryption and signatures and limit the use of these features to the subset that really requires such
a high level of security.

Encryption is known to be a lengthy process and hardware assist functions exist. However,
in a SOAP XML payload not all of the message will be encrypted, so an additional parsing
process is needed to delimit the boundaries of the encrypted data.

Similarly, the signature of an XML payload requires first the XML Canonicalization and
SOAP normalization of the messages to ensure that serialization processes do not add to the message extra spaces or line breaks that have no meaning. This XML Canonicalization process ends
up parsing the full XML message before attempting to compute a signature.

The impact on the processing time of a message can be up to one order of magnitude in the
worst cases.

Similarly, the signature itself can be disproportionate compared with the signed information as the headers have to include information on the selected Canonicalization method, tokens (such as X509) used for the signature, and the signature itself.

It is common to have 3,000 bytes of signature headers with tokens, certificate, and signature added to the message where the payload is only 100 bytes of information containing an account and amounts.[16]

Summary

We saw in this chapter that the life cycle management and runtime monitoring are flexible and dynamic processes, and that the services and application environment requires global and specific layer management operations. It should be noted, however, that the end-to-end business application process monitoring can be implemented without any explicit corresponding choreography, given that the correct event strategy has been applied across the various application and process domains. This monitoring is in the end what enables the enterprise to take the appropriate decisions that are essential in today's volatile economy.

Ad-hoc, event-driven, nondeterministic process management and monitoring is still a problem, as no monitoring model can be built due to the nondeterministic nature of the process. Correlation elements from the information model and time stamps can be a way to create on-the-fly monitoring models.

We have now reached the end of the book, and while I am conscious that more detail can always be provided, I hope that I've shared enough of my experience here that as you close this chapter, you are able to deliver more flexible and dynamic SOA and BPM implementations and control their life cycles.

Endnotes

Chapter 1

[1] Wikipedia Enterprise Architecture, http://en.wikipedia.org/wiki/Enterprise_Architecture.

[2] The Open Group, http://www.opengroup.org/.

[3] Zachman Framework, http://www.zachmaninternational.com/index.php/the-zachman-framework.

[4] Telemanagement Forum eTOM standard, http://www.tmforum.org/BestPracticesStandards/NGOSS BusinessProcess/1648/Home.html.

[5] APQC portal process classification framework, http://www.apqc.org/portal/apqc/site/?path=/research/pcf/index.html.

[6] IBM Component Business Modeling, http://www-935.ibm.com/services/us/gbs/bus/html/bcs_componentmodeling.html.

[7] MIT Sloan School of Management, A Coordination-Theoretic Approach to Understanding Process Differences, http://mitsloan.mit.edu/pdf/process-differences.pdf.

[8] Telco Application Map Standard from Telemanagement Forum, http://www.tmforum.org/page33552.aspx.

[9] OGSI Globus Grid Services Toolkit, http://www.globus.org/toolkit/.

[10] IBM SOA Foundation: An architectural introduction and overview 12, http://www.ibm.com/developerworks/webservices/library/ws-soa-whitepaper/.

[11] The RFC 3444, http://tools.ietf.org/html/rfc3444, titled "On the Difference between Information Models and Data Models," states the main purpose of an IM is to model managed objects at a conceptual level, independent of any specific implementations.

[12] BPMN specification 1.1, http://www.bpmn.org/Documents/BPMN%201-1%20Specification.pdf.

[13] Open SOA Collaboration, http://www.osoa.org.

Chapter 2

[1] IBM CICS transactional server, http://www-01.ibm.com/software/htp/cics/.

[2] Open SOA Collaboration, http://www.osoa.org.

[3] Telemanagement Forum eTOM reference, http://www.tmforum.org/browse.aspx?catID=1647.

[4] APQC portal process classification framework, http://www.apqc.org/portal/apqc/site/?path=/research/pcf/index.html.

[5] BPMN Private and Abstract processes page 13 and Figure 7.1 and 7.2 of www.bpmn.org/Documents/BPMN%201-1%20Specification.pdf.

[6] XPDL presentation, www.xpdl.org/tdocs/200809_KMWorld/200809_SJ04_XPDL_BPMN.ppt.

[7] WebSphere Business Modeler XML schema reference, http://publib.boulder.ibm.com/infocenter/dmndhelp/v6r1mx/index.jsp?topic=/com.ibm.btools.help.modeler.basic.doc/doc/reference/mappings/xmlschemareference.html.

[8] BPEL for People, http://download.boulder.ibm.com/ibmdl/pub/software/dw/specs/ws-bpel4people/BPEL4People_v1.pdf.

[9] Reference for <tag/> as the short form of an empty <tag></tag>, http://www.w3.org/TR/2008/REC-xml-20081126/#dt-empty.

Chapter 3

[1] U.S. government trademarks statistics, http://www.uspto.gov/web/offices/com/annual/2007/50319_table19.html.

[2] U.S. Census bureau statistics, http://www.census.gov/csd/susb/susb06.htm.

[3] IBM announcement letters, http://www-01.ibm.com/common/ssi/index.wss.

[4] U.S. Federal Data Reference Model, http://www.whitehouse.gov/omb/egov/documents/DRM_2_0_Final.pdf.

[5] IBM Financial Services models, https://www-03.ibm.com/industries/financialservices/doc/content/bin/fss_bdw_gim_0306.pdf.

[6] Telemanagement Forum Information Framework (SID), http://www.tmforum.org/DocumentsInformation/1696/home.html.

[7] RDF Vocabulary Description Language, http://www.w3.org/TR/rdf-schema/.

[8] Rational Fabric tooling for UML to OWL, http://www.ibm.com/developerworks/rational/downloads/08/rsa_webmodtool/index.html.

[9] URI RFC standard, http://www.rfc-editor.org/rfc/rfc3305.txt.

[10] ISO 20022 Universal financial industry message scheme, http://www.iso20022.org/.

[11] XML Linking Language (XLink), http://www.w3.org/TR/xlink/.

[12] IBM Sec Filing, http://www.sec.gov/Archives/edgar/data/51143/000110465908071167/ibm-20081028.xml.

[13] IBM Master Data Management, http://www-01.ibm.com/software/data/ips/products/masterdata/.

[14] Relationships in WebSphere, http://www.ibm.com/developerworks/websphere/library/techarticles/0605_lainwala/0605_lainwala.html.

[15] Services Data Object standard, http://www.osoa.org/display/Main/Service+Data+Objects+Home.

[16] Introduction to Service Data Objects, http://www.ibm.com/developerworks/java/library/j-sdo/.

[17] Adaptive Business Objects, http://www.research.ibm.com/people/p/prabir/ABO.pdf.

Chapter 4

[1] W3C Web Services home, http://www.w3.org/2002/ws/Activity.

[2] Erich Gamma et al., *Design Patterns: Elements of Reusable Object-Oriented Software*, (Addison-Wesley, 1995) ISBN-13: 978-0201633610.

[3] WSDL standard, http://www.w3.org/TR/wsdl.

[4] WS-I Basic Profile, http://www.ws-i.org/Profiles/BasicProfile-1.0-2004-04-16.html.

[5] WS-I Attachment profile, http://www.ws-i.org/Profiles/AttachmentsProfile-1.0.html.

[6] Open SOA SCA C++ binding,
http://www.osoa.org/download/attachments/28/SCA_ClientAndImplementationModel_Cpp_V09.pdf?
version=1.

[7] OMG's CORBA Interface Definition Language, http://www.omg.org/cgi-bin/doc?formal/02-06-39.

[8] Obtaining the WSDL for a PHP SCA component offering, http://www.php.net/manual/en/SCA.examples.
obtaining-wsdl.php.

[9] Open SOA SCA with PHP, http://www.osoa.org/display/PHP/SCA+with+PHP.

[10] Fielding's dissertation on Restful services, http://www.ics.uci.edu/~fielding/pubs/dissertation/
rest_arch_style.htm.

[11] IETF HTTP 1.1 Hypertext Transfer Protocol standard, http://tools.ietf.org/html/rfc2616.

Chapter 5

[1] ObjectWeb fractal model, http://fractal.objectweb.org/documentation.html.

[2] Definition of rete: synonym of plexus, http://wordnetweb.princeton.edu/perl/webwn?s=rete.

[3] Telemanagement Forum MTOSI standard, http://www.tmforum.org/mTOPMTOSIDocuments/2320/home.html.

Chapter 6

[1] Open SOA SCA Java Connector Architecture binding,
http://www.osoa.org/download/attachments/35/SCA_JCABindings_V1_00.pdf?version=2.

[2] WebSphere Dynamic Process Edition, http://www-01.ibm.com/software/integration/wdpe/.

[3] Zapthink SOA Software Forms an ESB Federation, http://www.zapthink.com/news.html?id=1949.

[4] WebSphere DataPower SOA Appliances, http://www-01.ibm.com/software/integration/datapower/.

[5] WebSphere Business Services Fabric, http://www-01.ibm.com/software/integration/wbsf/index.html.

[6] OWL Web Ontology Language, http://www.w3.org/TR/owl-features/.

[7] ILOG JRules, http://www.ilog.com/products/jrules/.

[8] JSR 94 Rules engine API, http://jcp.org/aboutJava/communityprocess/final/jsr094/index.html.

[9] ThreadLocal, http://java.sun.com/j2se/1.5.0/docs/api/java/lang/ThreadLocal.html.

[10] WebSphere Infocenter description of the Work Area Service, http://publib.boulder.ibm.com/infocenter/wasinfo/
v6r1/topic/com.ibm.websphere.express.doc/info/exp/workarea/concepts/cwa_overview.html.

[11] Building an aggregation function using WebSphere ESB, http://www.ibm.com/developerworks/websphere/
library/techarticles/0708_butek/0708_butek.html.

[12] IA12: WebSphere Message Brokers for z/OS - CICSRequest node, http://www-01.ibm.com/support/docview.wss?rs=171&uid=swg24006950&loc=en_US&cs=utf-8&lang=en.

Chapter 7

[1] Australian Government Standard Business Reporting Glossary, http://www.sbr.gov.au/content/taxonomy_glossary.htm.

[2] Common Information Model for Energy and Utilities, http://cimug.ucaiug.org/default.aspx.

[3] Telemanagement Forum Information Framework (SID), http://www.tmforum.org/DocumentsInformation/1696/home.html.

[4] ACORD Insurance Data Standard, http://www.acord.org/home/.

[5] Telemanagement Forum clickable business process framework, http://www.tmforum.org/BusinessProcessFramework/6775/home.html.

[6] WS-BPEL 2.0 Standard, http://docs.oasis-open.org/wsbpel/2.0/wsbpel-v2.0.html.

[7] Open SOA SCA standard, http://www.osoa.org/display/Main/Home.

[8] WS-BusinessActivity standard, http://docs.oasis-open.org/ws-tx/wstx-wsba-1.1-spec-errata-os.pdf.

Chapter 8

[1] IBM WebSphere Business Service Fabric Modeling Tool, http://www.ibm.com/developerworks/rational/downloads/08/rsa_webmodtool/index.html.

[2] WebSphere Registry and Repository Impact analysis, http://publib.boulder.ibm.com/infocenter/sr/v6r0/index.jsp?topic=/com.ibm.sr.doc/twsr_mansrvce_governanceuserguide02.html.

[3] Web Services Reliable Messaging, http://docs.oasis-open.org/ws-rx/wsrm/200608.

[4] Web Services Business Activity (WS-BusinessActivity), http://xml.coverpages.org/wstx-wsba-1.1-rddl.html.

[5] WebSphere Service Registry and Repository V6.0 documentation, http://publib.boulder.ibm.com/infocenter/sr/v6r0/index.jsp?topic=/com.ibm.sr.doc/twsr_mansrvce_coreuserguide103.html.

[6] WebSphere Business Process Engine API, http://publib.boulder.ibm.com/infocenter/dmndhelp/v6r2mx/index.jsp?topic=/com.ibm.websphere.wbpmcore.javadoc.620.doc/web/apidocs/com/ibm/bpe/api/package-summary.html.

[7] ITCAM for SOA, http://publib.boulder.ibm.com/infocenter/tivihelp/v3r1/index.jsp?topic=/com.ibm.itcamsoa.doc/kd4ugmst180.htm.

[8] User Defined XPath Function (UDXF) in WebSphere Business Monitor, http://www.ibm.com/developerworks/library/i-bam617/.

[9] IBM DataPower appliances, http://www-01.ibm.com/software/integration/datapower/.

[10] OASIS WSFED technical committee, http://www.oasis-open.org/committees/documents.php?wg_abbrev=wsfed.

[11] Liberty Alliance ID-FF, http://www.projectliberty.org/resource_center/specifications/liberty_alliance_id_ff_1_2_specifications.

[12] SAML, http://www.oasis-open.org/committees/tc_home.php?wg_abbrev=security.

[13] Understanding SOA Security Design and Implementation, http://www.redbooks.ibm.com/abstracts/sg247310.html.

[14] WebSphere Process Server end-to-end security tutorial, http://publib.boulder.ibm.com/infocenter/dmndhelp/v6r1mx/index.jsp?topic=/com.ibm.websphere.wps.612.doc/doc/tsec_endtoend.html.

[15] Audit trail in WebSphere Process Server, http://publib.boulder.ibm.com/infocenter/dmndhelp/v6r1mx/index.jsp?topic=/com.ibm.websphere.bpc.612.doc/doc/bpc/rg5attbl.html.

[16] CICS Transaction Server example of a signed SOAP message, http://publib.boulder.ibm.com/infocenter/cicsts/v3r2/index.jsp?topic=/com.ibm.cics.ts.webservices.doc/wsSecurity/dfhws_soapmsg_signed.html.

Index

A

ABOs (Adaptive Business Objects), 62

abstract processes, BPMN, 14-15, 32

abstract processes dynamic binding approach, 159

ACORD (Association for Cooperative Operations Research and Development), 127

activities, WS-BPEL, 140

actors, defined, 29

ad-hoc polymorphism
operation patterns (WSDL), variability, 66-67

adaptation, dynamic adaptation (ESBs), 101

adapter pattern, 63

Adaptive Business Objects (ABOs), 62

adding business semantics in bus meditations, 105

AggregateControl, 111

AggregateReply, 111

AggregateRequest, 111

aggregation
WebSphere DataPower, 111-112
WebSphere ESB, 110-111
WebSphere Message Broker, 111

agility
enterprise business agility, 24-25
enterprise technical agility, 22-23

allocating use cases, into process tree decomposition, 81-86

American Productivity and Quality Center. *See* APQC (American Productivity and Quality Center), 5

annotating code for service exposure
SCA (Service Component Architecture), 73-74

"any," variability, 52

application components, as private processes, 86-89

application layers, modeling, 127-131

application management layer, operational management, 162

Applications layer (enterprise architecture), 10-11
TmForum Telecom Applications Map, 11

FREE Online Edition

Your purchase of **Dynamic SOA and BPM** includes access to a free online edition for 120 days through the Safari Books Online subscription service. Nearly every IBM Press book is available online through Safari Books Online, along with more than 5,000 other technical books and videos from publishers such as Addison-Wesley Professional, Cisco Press, Exam Cram, O'Reilly, Prentice Hall, Que, and Sams.

SAFARI BOOKS ONLINE allows you to search for a specific answer, cut and paste code, download chapters, and stay current with emerging technologies.

Activate your FREE Online Edition at www.informit.com/safarifree

> **STEP 1:** Enter the coupon code: JDBVNCB.

> **STEP 2:** New Safari users, complete the brief registration form.
>   Safari subscribers, just log in.

If you have difficulty registering on Safari or accessing the online edition, please e-mail customer-service@safaribooksonline.com